Introdu

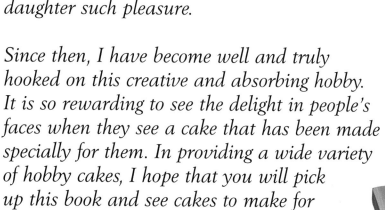

I made my first novelty cake just over five years ago for my daughter's 2nd birthday. The cake itself was a bit of a disaster: I had not allowed myself enough time nor having been introduced to smoothers! Nevertheless, I really enjoyed making something that gave my young daughter such pleasure.

Since then, I have become well and truly hooked on this creative and absorbing hobby. It is so rewarding to see the delight in people's faces when they see a cake that has been made specially for them. In providing a wide variety of hobby cakes, I hope that you will pick up this book and see cakes to make for your family and friends. Also I hope this book will give you the confidence to experiment with new techniques and designs and that you will take inspiration from the Special Effects sections to create your very own masterpieces!

Contents

HOW TO USE THIS BOOK

As you are reading through an article, you will find references to Special Effects sections.

These are marked with the code S.E. plus the relevant page number(s).

For example, in Cars, you will see S.E.p.15: this indicates that the special effect will be found in the Special Effects section on page 15.

£6·99

HOBBY
CAKES

PUBLISHING

Foreword

I am delighted to be able to contribute, in a very small way, to a book that I know will become a "must have" for anyone interested in cake decorating and sugarcraft.

This book is proof of Lindy's extraordinary talent, not only offering the readers the opportunity to recreate the author's own exceptional work, but also giving them the chance to adapt it according to personal requirements. Lindy's keen powers of observation and fertile imagination bring a fresh, vibrant approach to all her projects, while her use of colour is innovative and its effects stunning.

Tombi Peck
A founder member of the
British Sugarcraft Guild

First Published 2000 by B. Dutton Publishing Limited
Alfred House, Hones Business Park, Farnham, Surrey GU9 8BB
Copyright© Lindy Smith 2000
ISBN: 0-9532588-1-5
All rights reserved.

Lindy Smith has asserted her right under the Copyright, Designs and Patents Act, 1988, to be identified as the Author of this Work.
Publisher: Beverley Dutton • Editor: Rebecca Breuer • Design: Lorna Cowan • Photography: Alister Thorpe

Printed in England

Suppliers

Confectionery Supplies
Unit 11
Foley Trading Estate
Hereford HR1 2SF
Tel: 01432 371451
Shop, school and trade supplier.

Corteil & Barratt
40 High Street
Ewell Village
Surrey KT17 1RW
Tel: 020 8393 0032
Shop and school.

Culpitt Cake Art
Jubilee Industrial Estate
Ashington
Northumberland NE63 8UQ
01670 814545
Manufacturers and wholesale suppliers
of cake decorating and sugarcraft
equipment and decorations.

Great Impressions
Greenlea
14 Studley Drive
Swarland, Morpeth
Northumberland NE65 9JT
Tel: 01670 787061
Veiners (a speciality), moulds and
transfers.
Mail order.

Guy, Paul & Co.
Unit B4
Foundry Way
Little End Road
Eaton Socon
Cambridgeshire
PE19 3JH
01480 472545
Trade suppliers of tools
and materials for the
art of bakery, sugarcraft
and food decoration.

Holly Products
Holly Cottage
Hassall Green
Sandbach
Cheshire
CW11 4YA
Tel: 01270 761403
Moulds, embossers,
patterns and tools.
Mail order.

Orchard Products
51 Hallyburton Road
Hove
East Sussex
BN3 7GP
Tel: 01273 419418
Manufacturers and
suppliers of fine
quality sugarcraft cutters
and tools.
Shop and mail order.

Squires Kitchen Sugarcraft
Squires House
3 Waverley Lane
Farnham
Surrey
GU9 8BB
Tel: 01252 711749
Sugarcraft colours, tools, equipment,
marzipans and sugarpastes.
Shop, school, mail order, manufacturer
and wholesaler.

Publications

Squires Kitchen Magazine
Publishing Ltd.
Alfred House
Hones Business Park
Farnham
Surrey
GU9 8BB
Tel: 01252 727572
Publishers of CAKES & Sugarcraft
Magazine, a monthly title offering new
ideas and inspirations to the
sugarcrafter.

Merehurst
Ferry House
51-57 Lacy Road
Putney
London
SW15 1PR
Tel: 020 8355 1480
Publishers of many cake decorating
and sugarcraft titles.

Societies

The British Sugarcraft Guild
Wellington House
Messeter Place
Eltham
London SE9 5DP
Tel: 020 8859 6943

Acknowledgements

With thanks to my family and friends for their
interest, encouragement and valued opinions.

This book is dedicated to my
husband, Graham, and to my
two children, Charlotte and Tristan.

Basic Recipes

Madeira Cake
As a firm but moist cake, this is ideal for novelty work.

1. *Pre-heat the oven to 160°C /325°F/Gas 3.*

2. *Grease and line the cake tin (pan).*

3. *Cream the butter and sugar in a large mixing bowl until light, fluffy and very pale.*

4. *Sift the flours together into a bowl. Beat the eggs one at a time into the creamed mixture, following each with a spoonful of flour to prevent the mixture from curdling.*

5. *Sift the remaining flour into the creamed mix and fold in carefully with a large metal spoon.*

6. *Transfer the mixture into the prepared cake tin (pan) and bake. Baking times will depend very much on your oven, the cake tin used and the depth of the cake. I usually check the cake after 1-1$^1/_4$ hours, depending on its size. If the cake is baked, it will be well risen, firm to the touch and a skewer inserted into the centre will come out clean.*

7. *Allow the cake to cool then, without removing the lining paper, wrap the cake in foil or place in an airtight container for at least 12 hours before cutting to allow the cake to settle.*

Buttercream
Buttercream is used throughout this book both to sandwich cakes together and to coat them before covering with sugarpaste. You will find that, as you spread the buttercream over the sponge, it will fill any holes to give a smooth surface on which to apply the sugarpaste.

Ingredients
110g/ 4oz/$^1/_2$ cup butter
1-2 tablespoons milk or water
340g/12oz/2$^1/_2$ cups icing (confectioners') sugar
A few drops of vanilla extract

Method
1. *Place the butter in a bowl and beat until light and fluffy*

2. *Sift the icing sugar into the bowl and continue to beat until the mixture changes colour. Add just enough milk or water to give a firm but spreadable consistency.*

3. *Flavour by adding the vanilla, then store in an airtight container until required.*

Modelling Paste
As its name suggests, this paste is used for modelling: it keeps its shape well and dries harder than sugarpaste. Squires Kitchen manufactures a ready-made Mexican Modelling Paste (MMP) available from specialist sugarcraft shops. Alternatively, you may wish to make your own using one of the following methods:

1. *EITHER: Knead equal quantities of sugarpaste and flowerpaste together. The proportion of sugarpaste to flowerpaste can be adjusted for softer or firmer pastes.*

2. OR: *Knead 1 teaspoon of gum tragacanth, a natural gum available from cake decorating suppliers, into 225g (8oz) sugarpaste. Wrap in a plastic bag and allow to the gum to work before use. You will begin to feel a difference in the paste after an hour or so. (This is my preferred method.)*

Flowerpaste (Squires Kitchen Sugar Florist Paste (SFP))

Flowerpaste is available commercially and is used either for making superfine sugar flowers or for fine modelling. It is particularly useful for clothing figures as it can be rolled translucently thin and will then behave in a similar fashion to material. Like sugarpaste, flowerpaste can be purchased in white or in an ever-increasing variety of colours. I find the dark colours such as black, brown and dark blue particularly useful.

Sugarpaste

Ready-made sugarpaste is readily available in supermarkets and from cake decorating suppliers and is available in white and the whole colour spectrum. White paste allows you to produce your own colours (see Colour Mixing on page 9), whilst ready-coloured paste, particularly red and black, are very useful.

Sugar Glue

Although sugar glue is now commercially available, it is quick and easy to make at home. There are many ways to do this and, if you are an experienced sugarcrafter, you will probably have a preferred method.

I make sugar glue as follows: Break up a piece of white modelling paste approximately the size of a large marble into an egg cup and fill with boiling water. Allow the water to dissolve the paste, stirring occasionally to quicken the process. This produces thick strong glue, which can, if required, easily be thinned by adding cooled boiled water. If a really strong glue is required, use pastillage as the base in place of the modelling paste.

Sugar Sticks

These are inserted into models to give support (see Figure Modelling on pages 92-93). They are a sugar alternative to spaghetti and very easy to make.

Place some of the soft pastillage (as mentioned later) into a sugar shaper fitted with a small round disc and extrude lengths onto foam. Straighten and leave overnight to dry thoroughly. Snap the lengths into suitable sizes and store until required .

Pastillage

This is an extremely useful paste because, unlike modelling paste, it sets extremely hard. There are many recipes for pastillage: the one described below is the one I have used for creating the cakes in this book. NOTE: If you are concerned about using raw egg white, Squires Kitchen Pastillage is available in

powder form to which you simply add water. This contains pasteurised egg white.

Ingredients
1 egg white
280g/10oz/$2^{1}/_{4}$ cups sifted icing (confectioners') sugar
2 teaspoons gum tragacanth

Method
1. *Put the egg white into a large mixing bowl and gradually add enough icing sugar to make a very stiff royal icing. Mix in the gum tragacanth, then turn the paste out onto the work surface and knead together.*

2. *If you require some softer pastillage to make items with a sugar shaper, place some to one side (see note), then incorporate the remaining icing sugar into the rest to give a stiff paste.*

NOTE: *Pastillage should be stored in a polythene bag and placed in an airtight container.*

Madeira Cake Quantities

CAKES	PAGES	BAKEWARE	EGGS (medium)	BUTTER	CASTER SUGAR (superfine)	SELF RAISING FLOUR	PLAIN FLOUR (all purpose)	BAKING TIMES @ 160°C/325°F
Birdwatching	66-71	1¼ litre/2 pint pudding basin	3	170g/6oz/¾ cup	170g/6oz/¾ cup	170g/6oz/½ cup	85g/3oz/¾ cup	1 - 1¼ hours
Mountain Biking	46-49	20cm/8" round tin	5	280g/10oz/1¼ cups	280g/10oz/1¼ cups	280g/10oz/2½ cups	140g/5oz/1¼ cups	1 - 1¼ hours
Home Brewing	34-37	3 x 10cm/4" round and 12.5cm/5" square tins						
Cars	10-15	23cm/9" square tin	6	340g/12oz/1½ cups	340g/12oz/1½ cups	340g/12oz/3 cups	170g/6oz/1½ cups	1 - 1¼ hours
Walking	16-19	15cm x 30cm/6" x 12" oblong tin						
Fishing	24-29							
Golf	38-41	25.5cm/10" round tin						
Darts	30-33							
DIY	20-23	2 x 15cm/6" round tins						
Ballooning	62-65							
Cooking	42-45	2 x 18cm/7" round tins	7	400g/14oz/1¾ cups	400g/14oz/1¾ cups	400g/14oz/3½ cups	200g/7oz/1¾ cups	1¼ hours
Horse Riding	50-55	2 x 15cm/6" square tins						1¼ - 1½ hours
Sugarcraft	80-85	20cm/8" square tin						
Karting	86-91	30cm x 15cm/12" x 6" oblong and 8cm/3¼" round tins.						1 hour
Crosswords	76-79	23cm x 28cm/9" x 11" oblong tin	8	450g/1lb/2 cups	450g/1lb/2 cups	450g/1lb/4 cups	225g/8oz/2 cups	1¼ hours
Gardening	56-61	2 x 18cm /7" square tins	10	560g/1lb 4oz/2½ cups	560g/1lb 4oz/2½ cups	560g/1lb 4oz/5 cups	280g/10oz/2½ cups	1¼ hours
Computers	72-75	2 x 20cm/8" square tins	11	620g/1lb 6oz/2¾ cups	620g/1lb 6oz/2¾ cups	620g/1lb 6oz/5½ cups	310g/1lb 11oz/2¾ cups	1¼ hours

Lindy's Tips

✿ It is often advisable to carve a cake from frozen, as this will give you a much firmer base on which to work and help to prevent the cake from crumbling.

✿ When figure modelling, remember to allow yourself sufficient time. It is advisable to allow the figure to dry thoroughly before dressing him: a week in a warm, dry place would be ideal.

✿ Designed specifically for use with metallic lustre dust colours, Squires Kitchen Gildesol is an edible gilding medium that is very easy to use. Simply work a small amount of Gildesol over the surface of the sugarwork with a soft-bristled brush, apply the lustre dust colour, puff away any excess and burnish with a clean soft brush. Gildesol also intensifies the colour of and gives a lustrous finish to non-metallic dust ranges.

✿ It is advisable to use paste colours rather than liquid colours when colouring sugarpaste, modelling paste or flowerpaste. Even so, you will find that when vivid or dark colours are required, a lot of paste colour is needed; this can make the paste quite sticky. To overcome this problem, add a pinch or two of gum tragacanth to sugarpaste and a small amount of white fat to flowerpaste. The gum will make the paste firmer and easier to handle.

✿ Use smoothers to achieve a professional finish on a sugarpasted cake.

✿ Use spacers to achieve an even thickness when rolling out paste. These are available commercially, but you can make your own (from strip wood available from DIY stores, for example).

✿ Invest in a sugar shaper. In my opinion, a sugar shaper is indispensable for novelty work, as the assortment of interchangeable discs means that it can be used to make many items (e.g. hair, grass, posts, poles). NOTE: The secret to using a sugar shaper successfully is to make sure that the paste used is really soft. I find that adding cooled boiled water to the paste until it just starts to stick to my hands ensures that the paste will be extruded quickly and easily.

✿ Cutting wheels are excellent for cutting rolled out pastillage and flowerpaste as they do not pull or drag the paste.

Colour Mixing

When colouring sugarpaste, modelling paste or flowerpaste, it helps to be aware of the basics of colour theory. The colour wheel is the best guide to this as it features all the colours of the rainbow, i.e. the three primary and three secondary (indigo and violet are combined as purple) colours.

☐ Primary Colours

So called because they cannot be created by mixing other colours together. Primary colours are essential for anyone wishing to colour paste themselves, especially as it is from these colours that all other colours are made.

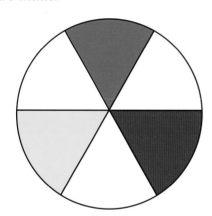

◯ Secondary Colours

Secondary colours are made by mixing two primary colours together in equal amounts:

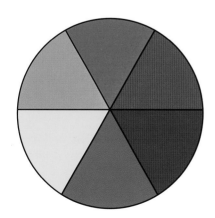

Browns

To mix brown, either mix all the primary colours together or mix a secondary colour with the primary colour that lies opposite it on the colour wheel:

Black

Adding small amounts of black to a colour will mute it, making it less garish (I added black to many of the colours used in the Fishing cake, for example).

Have a go and have fun experimenting: you will be amazed at some of the wonderful colours you can prepare.

Colouring Paste

To colour sugarpaste, modelling paste or flowerpaste, place a little paste colour on the end of a cocktail stick. Add it to the paste and knead in thoroughly. Keep adding more colour a little at a time until you achieve the required shade. NOTE: The paste will appear a slightly darker colour when dry.

Materials

6 egg Madeira cake cooked in a 23cm
(9") square tin
Buttercream
1.63kg (4lb 10oz) sugarpaste,
coloured as follows:
450g (1lb) white
450g (1lb) red
280g (10oz) black
672g (1½lb) grey
225g (8oz) to make the gravel
(to be coloured as desired)
573g (1lb 4½oz) Mexican Modelling
Paste (MMP), coloured as follows:
280g (10oz) black
196g (7oz) white
15g (½oz) yellow, 54g (2oz) green
28g (1oz) red
Flowerpaste:
28g (1oz) green (for the bucket)
28g (1oz) black (for the roof)
28g (1oz) white (for the roof)
28g (1oz) yellow (for the chamois
and book)
Paste colours to colour the above:
red (SK Christmas Red)
yellow (SK Sunflower)
brown (SK Chestnut)
green (SK Mint)
black
Squires Kitchen Edible Lustre Dusts:
Silver and Snowflake
Clear spirit, e.g. gin or vodka
White fat, e.g. Trex or White Flora
Sugar glue

Equipment

30.5cm x 25.5cm (12" x 10")
oval board, Large knife
Small palette knife
Cutting wheel
Set square, Paintbrushes
Circle cutters: 2cm (¾")
4cm (1½"), 5cm (2")
Sugar shaper
Narrow strip cutter
Waxed paper, Craft knife
Dresden tool, Sieve, Cocktail sticks
Spacers, Smoother, Ribbon
Food pens: red, black and green

TEMPLATES USED

Ever since the first cars were produced in the latter half of the 19th century, people have been captivated and fascinated by them. In the 1890s, cars were largely recreational vehicles for the wealthy. Henry Ford, however, made cars more widely available when he started to produce his model T in 1908. Today cars are our main form of transport, with the total number in use worldwide estimated at around half a billion. Cars also form the basis of many people's hobbies, for example racing, rallying, collecting cars and car memorabilia, restoring old models and building kit cars. The possibilities for this cake were endless, but I decided to portray a much-loved car being washed and waxed. Why not adapt my design to make the car of your choice?

Covering the Board

Make the gravel and allow to dry (S.E.p.15).

Cover the board with the grey sugarpaste. Once dry, paint sugar glue over the surface and sprinkle on the gravel. Level it slightly with a smoother and place to one side.

The Wheels

Roll out the black modelling paste to a height of 1.5cm (5/8") and cut five wheels (four plus the spare) using the 4cm (1¾") circle cutter. Place the smallest circle cutter in the centre of a wheel and, with a craft knife, remove some of the paste inside the cutter. Remove the cutter and repeat for the other wheels. Add the tread to each wheel (S.E.p.15) and allow to dry. Thickly roll out some white modelling paste and cut five hubcaps with the smallest circle cutter. Shape them so that they become slightly domed, then glue one to the centre of each wheel.

Carving the Cake

TIP: Having a toy car to look at when carving the car is invaluable, as it is much easier to compare the shape of the cake with a 3-dimentional object than a 2-dimentional picture.

10

1. Level the cake and cut it vertically in half. Stack the resulting rectangles on top of one another, securing them together with buttercream. Cut the crusts off one side so that the car has a width of 9.5cm (3¾").

TIP: You will probably find it best to freeze the cake at this stage

and then carve it from frozen, as this will give you a much firmer base on which to work.

2. Prepare two car templates (see page 96) and, using cocktail sticks, pin them either side of the stacked cakes. Then, with a large knife, cut around the bonnet, roof and boot of the car.

3. To cut the base, place the cake on one side, then slice into the cake along the line shown on the template to a depth of 2cm (¾"). Turn the cake over and repeat, then remove similar amounts of cake from underneath the bonnet and boot. Next, take the largest circle cutter and remove the cake from the wheel arches.

4. Remove the templates and start to shape the car by carefully cutting and shaping the sides and bonnet, then carving the boot, windscreen, rear window and roof. Remove only small amounts of cake at a time and use the photographs and, preferably, a toy car as guides.

5. Place the carved cake on waxed paper.

Covering the Cake

1. Spread a thin layer of buttercream around the base of the car and in the wheel arches. Roll out some black sugarpaste to cover ¼ of the base (from one wheel arch to the next), carefully position the paste and trim to shape. Repeat for the next wheel arch to wheel arch section, rubbing over the join in the paste to close. Continue until the base is covered.

2. Spread buttercream over the remaining uncovered cake and cover with a thin layer of white sugarpaste. Trim this paste where it meets the black base with a small palette knife; also, trim the wheel arches with the largest circle cutter. Smooth the paste with a smoother.

NOTE: This layer of paste gives you a firmer base on which to work. It also allows you easily to add pieces of sugarpaste, should you wish to alter or adjust the shape of the car slightly.

3. Cover the window area with black sugarpaste. Do this in four sections, cutting the paste so that the joins are at the corners. Rub the joins to close, then smooth. Brush some snowflake lustre dust over the windows and rub it in. Allow to dry.

4. Roll out some red sugarpaste between spacers and cut a 4cm (1½") wide rectangle to fit across the back window. Paint water or sugar glue around the outside of the window and place the paste in position. Trim the paste at the corners

of the car, then place the window template (No.1, page 96) centrally over the paste. With a cutting wheel or craft knife, cut carefully around the template. Remove the paste to reveal the window below. In a similar fashion, cover the side windows using 3.5cm (1³⁄₈") wide rectangles and the windscreen (Template 2, page 96) using a 4cm (1¹⁄₂") wide rectangle. Cut each to size and reveal the window as before.

5. To cover one side of the car, roll out a 5cm (2") wide rectangle and glue it in position under the windows. Smooth the join with a finger and the rest of the side with a smoother. Cut the paste to the sides along the lines of the body trim and, underneath, flush with the black paste. Cut out the wheel arches using the largest circle cutter. Mark the door with a cutting wheel, using a set square to ensure that the lines are vertical. Repeat for the other side.

6. Cover the back of the car in the same fashion, cutting it to fit with the sides and marking on the boot. To cover the front of the car, firstly place a 0.75cm (¹⁄₄") wide strip under the windscreen. Cover the wings and trim to size. Then cut some paste for the bonnet and glue in position.

7. To make the body trim, roll out some red sugarpaste and cut it into strips using a strip cutter. Paint lines of glue along the four joins in the bodywork and stick the strips in place. Roll out some white modelling paste and also cut it into strips. Paint glue around the inside edges of the windows and stick on the strips. Then stick similar strips along the sill and

over the wheel arches.

8. Using a craft knife, remove the paste where the front grill and the number plate on the boot will be. Roll out a small amount of white modelling paste, cut it to the size of the back number plate and insert it into position. Roll out some more modelling paste and indent it with the strip cutter, being careful not to cut all the way through. Place the grill template (No.3, page 96) on top, cut out the grill and stick it in position so that the lines are horizontal. Then cut further strips and place them vertically on and around the grill.

9. With some red paste, model a petrol cap, door and boot hinges and the first section of the front bumper. With black modelling paste, model the boot handle, windscreen wipers and spray nozzles. Then, with some white modelling paste, add the front and rear bumpers, front number plate and "L" plates, the base of the front headlights, indicator lights and rear lights, the boot keyhole and the door handles.

10. Dilute some silver lustre dust in clear spirit and carefully paint all of the white trimmings silver, excluding the number plates and "L" plates but including the hubcaps. You may need two coats.

11. Add the coloured lights and the white headlights, using a

kitchen sieve to texture them. Write the vehicle registration on the number plates with a black food pen (there is a lot of scope here for personalising your cake) and "L"s on the "L" plates with a red food pen.

12. Cover the roof of the car by cutting the appropriate shape from thickly rolled out white sugarpaste. Smooth the cut edges with fingers and the top with a smoother. Add a trim around the roof using strips cut with a strip cutter.

13. Once the roof has dried, mark on a chequered pattern with a craft knife: the squares should be approximately 1cm (³⁄₈") in size, but measure the roof to check. Thinly roll out the black and white flowerpastes and, with

a cutting wheel, cut into 1cm (³⁄₈") wide strips. Use these strips to make the chequered pattern, gluing and cutting them to size.

14. Place the cake on the board. Add the wheels to the car, securing them in place with balls of black paste. To make the car shine, apply a thin layer of Trex or White Flora over the roof, body and windows using a paintbrush.

Assembling the Cake

Make a bucket, a sponge and a tin of turtle wax, a chamios leather, a car manual, a tool box, a tool box tray and a jack (S.E.pp. 14-15). Position these accessories on the board, then make the hose by extruding a length of paste from a sugar shaper fitted with the small round disc and filled with softened yellow modelling paste. Finally, attach a ribbon around the board.

SPECIAL *Effects* & *Accessories*

Bucket

To make the bucket, roll out some green flowerpaste on a lightly greased board, then cut out a 2.5cm (1") x 8cm (3") rectangle and a 2cm (¾") circle. Allow the paste to harden slightly before picking up the rectangle and wrapping it around the circle, gluing the edges together. Once the bucket is dry, cut a thin strip of paste and glue into position for a handle.

Sponge & Turtle wax

Model the sponge and turtle wax tin from small amounts of modelling paste: decorate the tin with food pens.

Chamois Leather

Roll out some yellow flowerpaste very thinly and cut out a chamois leather. Place it on the roof so that it looks as though it has just been left there.

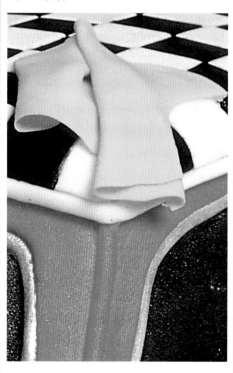

Car Manual

For the car manual, cut a 3.5cm x 2.5cm (1½" x 1") rectangle from yellow flowerpaste. Fold it in half, crease the fold, then open it up and place it on the bonnet. Allow it to firm up, then repeat with a slightly smaller rectangle of white flowerpaste. Indent all the edges with a craft knife to represent pages. Once dry, add the text and drawings with a food pen.

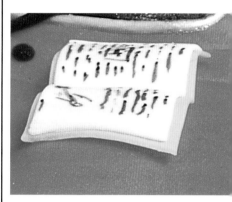

Toolbox

To make the toolbox, model an oblong (3.5cm (1½") long, 1.5cm (½") high and 1.5cm (½") wide) from green modelling paste. Model the lid as shown from black

modelling paste. Indent the top of the lid with a Dresden tool and place a small sausage of paste inside to represent the handle. Neaten the join between the lid

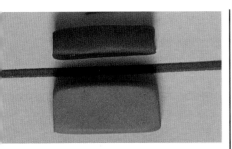

and the box by placing a strip of black paste over it. Attach a small ball of white paste to form a catch.

Tool Box Tray

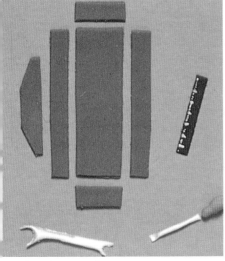

Make the tray by cutting a rectangle, slightly smaller than the interior dimensions of the tool box, from thinly rolled green modelling paste. Cut the sides and centre as illustrated. Allow to dry before sticking in position. Make some small tools to fit inside the tray from small amounts of flowerpaste as shown. Once the tools are dry, paint any metal parts with silver lustre dust mixed with clear spirit, then secure them in the tray with sugar glue.

Jack

Model the jack as shown: it has an overall length of 4cm (1½") and a maximum height of 1cm (⅜").

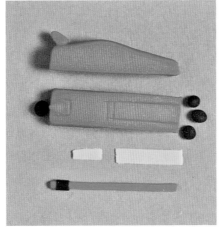

Gravel

Gravel is available in many colours, so it is entirely up to you which, and how many, colours you wish to use. I used white, a number of shades of grey, brown and a small amount of black. To make the gravel, thickly roll out some of the sugarpaste and cut it into strips and then cubes as illustrated.

Repeat with the other colours and allow to dry. Then place the cubes on a chopping board and, with a large sharp knife, cut them in different directions, as though you were chopping parsley. You are aiming to produce small angular pieces of paste.

Tyre Treads

The simplest way to make tread on tyres is to use clean, preferably sterilised, toy wheels from your (grand)children's vehicles: search through their toy boxes and see what you can find.

To make the tread, gently (but firmly) roll the plastic wheel around the edge of the paste wheel whilst it is still soft, then allow to dry. An alternative, if you don't have ready access to toy wheels, is to use modelling tools to indent the surface of the tyre: experiment and see what effects you can create with the tools you have. If you wish to accentuate the fine tread pattern on a tyre, rub a contrasting dust colour over the surface of the tread.

Materials

40.5cm x 35.5cm (16"x14") oval
cake drum
15cm x 30.5cm (6"x12") oblong
Madeira cake, Buttercream
2kg (4$\frac{1}{2}$lb) sugarpaste:
450g (1lb) black
900g (2lb) coloured various stone
colours
675g (1$\frac{1}{2}$lb) pale green
Sugar glue
323g (11$\frac{1}{2}$oz) Mexican Modelling
Paste (MMP):
280g (10oz) flesh
15g (1/2oz) red, 28g (1oz) brown
Flowerpaste (for dressing the figures):
28g (1oz) cream
15g ($\frac{1}{2}$oz) light brown
15g ($\frac{1}{2}$oz) orange (SK Nasturtium)
15g ($\frac{1}{2}$oz) red (SK Poinsettia)
15g ($\frac{1}{2}$oz) black
15g ($\frac{1}{2}$oz) dark brown (SK Bulrush)
28g (1oz) dark blue-green
28g (1oz) pale green
Paste colours:
Various greens (e.g. SK Forest Green,
Vine and
Christmas Green)
Assorted colours to paint the
faces & map
White (SK Edelweiss)
Clear spirit, e.g. gin or vodka
Dust colours:
Browns (SK Chestnut and Bulrush)
Greens (SK Shady Moss and
Lichen Glow)
Black (SK Smokey Haze)

Equipment

Stiff bristled kitchen brush, e.g.
bottle brush
Holly Products Adult Head Mould, Body
templates (see page 97), Sugar shaper
2cm ($\frac{3}{4}$") circle cutter
Fern cutter, Small pair of scissors
Cutting wheel
Paintbrushes, Stitching wheel
Pieces of foam (to support the figures)
Ribbed material (for texturing the socks)
Dresden tool, Piping tube: No. 0
Scouring pad, Craft knife, Ribbon

WALKING

Walking is the easiest, cheapest, most convenient and arguably the most effective long-term exercise of all. It is a totally natural activity which millions of us enjoy. So whether you are an everyday dog walker, weekend rambler or even if you only venture out walking occasionally, this could be the cake for you.

Carving the Cake

1. Level the cake to a height of 5cm (2") and reduce the depth by cutting it from 15cm (6") to 11.5cm (4$\frac{1}{2}$"). Place the cake on its long side and cut the opening in the wall, approximately 18cm (7") from one end (see Fig.1). Turn one piece over and place both pieces on the board to make the wall (see Figs.2 & 3). Cut the remaining cake into pieces and scatter them around the wall to give the impression of gently undulating ground.

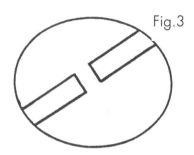

Fig.3

Covering the Cake

1. Spread a thin layer of buttercream over the wall and cover it with black sugarpaste. Next, spread buttercream over the rest of the cake and cover the scattered cake and board with green sugarpaste. Texture the grass with a stiff bristled kitchen brush (S.E.p.71) and allow to dry.

2. Model stones from the various stone-coloured pastes and glue them on top of the black wall. Model more stones in different

Fig.1

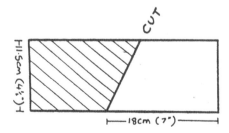

Fig.2

16

sizes and shapes, taking care to shape them around the corners of the wall so they have a solid appearance. Once the wall is covered, make the larger capping stones and the loose stones and arrange them on the cake.

3. Colour the stones as described (S.E.p.19), then paint the grass with a range of diluted green paste colours.

4. Make a map and a daypack (S.E.p.19).

The Figures

For detailed instructions on how to make the body parts, please refer to Figure Modelling on pages 92-93.

TIP: Although I have described how to make the figuresseparately, I would advise making them in tandem.

The Female Walker

1. *Torso:* Model the torso using the medium-sized female template (see page 94). Insert spaghetti through the body and place the torso at the foot of the wall, but do not secure in place.

2. *Legs:* Model the legs and attach them to the hips with sugar glue. Position the legs so that the right ankle rests on the left thigh and support in position with foam until dry. Once the paste holds its shape, remove the figure from the cake and place in a warm dry place, such as an airing cupboard, to dry thoroughly.

3. Make the head (using the medium-sized mould, see Figure Modelling on page 92), trousers (see Sugarcraft on page 82) and T-shirt body (see The Male Walker as below).

4. *Socks:* Wrap a 1cm ($^3/_8$") strip of red flowerpaste around the lower leg to give the socks more bulk. Next, thinly roll out some red flowerpaste, texture it with the narrow ribbed material and cut two 1.5cm ($^1/_2$") wide strips. Wrap these carefully around her ankles and lower legs, covering the strip beneath. Make the tops of the socks from 0.5cm ($^1/_4$") wide textured strips and secure in place. Press the sharp end of a Dresden tool along all the edges of the sock tops to neaten their appearance.

5. *Boots:* Make the tongues by gluing 0.75cm ($^1/_4$") wide strips of black flowerpaste centrally on top of the feet. Next, attach two 1cm ($^3/_8$") wide strips of brown flowerpaste on either side of the tongue of each boot. The strips should meet at the toe and heel and partially overlap the tongue. Add extra pieces of paste for the toecaps and trimmings of the boots as desired. Walking boots come in many designs and colours, so the choice is yours. Paint the soles of the feet with glue and stick on a ball of black flowerpaste that has been flattened to the appropriate shape. Indent the tread on each boot with a Dresden tool. Let down some of the black sugarpaste trimmings with cooled boiled water to a piping consistency and pipe the laces on each boot with a No. 0 tube.

6. *Arms:* Place the figure back in position on the cake. Model the arms and attach them to the body. Support the map on the figure's lap with foam, then position the hands so that they appear to be holding the map. Support each arm with foam and allow to dry.

7. Make the jacket, collar and cuffs (S.E.pp.68-69). Attach the head and make the hair (see page 93).

The Male Walker

1. *Torso:* Model the torso using the medium-sized male template (see page 97) and place it so that the body sits on the edge of the broken wall. Shape the torso so that he is leaning forward. Insert a length of spaghetti through his body into the wall to help give him support.

2. *Legs:* Model the legs and attach them to the hips. Position the legs using pieces of foam to give support.

3. Model the head (see Figure Modelling on page 92), the trousers (S.E.p.82) and the socks and boots as before.

4. Place the man back in position on the cake and make the arms. Attach to the body and position using pieces of foam.

5. *T-shirt Sleeves:* Cut two rectangles from thinly rolled cream flowerpaste. Paint sugar glue around the shoulders and under the armpits of the figure. Drape one rectangle over an arm and join the paste underneath to make the underarm seam. Trim this seam with scissors and cut off the excess paste at the shoulders with a cutting wheel. Repeat for the second sleeve.

6. *T-shirt Body:* Roll out a

18

rectangle of cream paste. Use the circle cutter to remove a half circle of paste to make the neck and cut away the armholes. Paint glue around the shoulders, arms and sides and place the front of the shirt in position, trimming it to shape at the shoulders and sides with a cutting wheel. Make the back in the same manner, ensuring the hem length is the same as the front.

7. Place a piece of foam on the wall behind the man so that you can place the daypack on his back. To make the pack's straps, cut strips from black flowerpaste and stick them in position. Attach the pack and allow to dry. Attach the head and make the hair.

Assembling the Cake
Model a water bottle from cream flowerpaste trimmings and paint on a blue colour wash to give the impression of water. Add a black cap. Cut some small fern leaves from pale green flowerpaste and, once they are dry, attach them to the board with let-down green sugarpaste. When secure, paint with diluted green paste colours. Colour some of the light green sugarpaste trimmings bright green. Place them in a sugar shaper together with a mesh disc and extrude tufts of grass. Randomly attach these to the board. Finally, secure the ribbon around the board.

SPECIAL *Effects* & *Accessories*

Map
Cut a 5cm x 7cm (2" x 2³⁄₄")

rectangle from cream flowerpaste. Leave it for about two minutes to become firmer, then make the creases by folding and unfolding the map in half, then quarters in both directions. Place the map on an uneven surface (e.g. a scrunched up plastic bag), arranging it to look as

though it is being held at the sides. Once dry, paint all the detail on the map with a fine paintbrush and very diluted paste colours. Make the map cover to ¹⁄₈ of the size of the map. Paint the detail and attach the cover to the underside of the top left hand corner of the map (see the main photograph).

Daypack
1. Make a 2.75cm (1") ball from red modelling paste and flatten it slightly on four sides to make the basic shape (see photograph). Allow to dry.

2. Cut a 6cm x 10cm (2¹⁄₄" x 4") rectangle from thinly rolled red flowerpaste. Paint glue on the top and base of the pack. Place a corner of the rectangle on the base, then pleat the paste around it so that it covers the

dried centre with some fullness. Cut the paste to size at the back of the pack and bring all the edges in at the top, cutting off the excess with scissors. Run a stitching wheel over the paste to form the four corner seams of the pack.

3. Make the front patch pocket

from a small flattened ball of paste and the top flap from thinly rolled paste cut to an appropriate size. Run the stitching wheel around each. Let down some of the black sugarpaste, trimming to a piping consistency, and pipe on the ties and zip with a No. 0 tube.

Dry Stone Walling
Dry stone walls are made from stones laid on top of one another without the use of mortar so, to recreate this in sugar, first cover the wall with black sugarpaste to represent the dark recesses of the wall. Once dry, model stones in various shapes, sizes and colours and glue them to the wall in rough layers. When dry, dust the stones with a mixture of green, brown and black dusts and stipple white lichen patches over some of the stones with undiluted white paste colour.

MORE SPECIAL *Effects*

Stone Walls
This example has been made by carefully pressing an impression mat on to soft sugarpaste and, once dry, dusting with a selection of coloured dusts. As you can see, the colours you choose greatly influence the overall appearance of the wall.

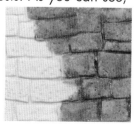

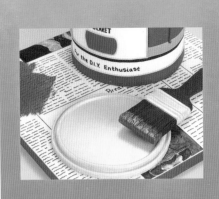

Materials

32.5cm (13") square cake drum
6 egg Madeira cake, cooked in two
15cm (6") round tins
Buttercream
2.24kg (5lb) sugarpaste
170g (6oz) pastillage
450g (1lb) Mexican Modelling
Paste (MMP)
Paste Colours: Black
Yellow (SK Sunflower)
Red (SK Christmas Red and
Cyclamen
Paint pot colours
Confectioners' glaze
Squires Kitchen Edible Lustre Dust:
Light Gold and Light Silver
Gildesol
Clear spirit, e.g. gin or vodka
Sugar glue

Equipment

Wooden dowel
Small cutting wheel (optional)
Foam (for drying the pastillage)
Former (for the paint tin handle)
Non-stick, non-absorbent material,
e.g. Bake-O-Glide
4mm spacers
Waxed paper
Paintbrushes
Newspaper (for reference)
Small palette knife
2mm strip cutter
Letter cutters
Ribbon

TEMPLATE USED

DIY-Painting

The term DIY first came into common usage in England in the 1950s. Before the Second World War, 70% of the population lived in rented accommodation, so there was no incentive to do-it-yourself; in fact, undertaking your own home improvements carried a social stigma.

After the war, however, labour prices rocketed and professional builders were fully employed in the rebuilding of Britain, so there was no alternative but to do-it-yourself. By the mid 1950s, manufacturers started to respond to this new trend by providing paints for the domestic market and by introducing new materials such as Formica and hardboard. What comprised a whole new industry 50 years ago has today become a part of the fabric of our lives: I am sure most of us at one time or another have picked up a paintbrush and helped to decorate a room.

Covering the Board

Colour 1kg (2lb) sugarpaste an off-white shade using a touch of black and yellow. Cover the board and allow to dry thoroughly. For the newsprint design, cut out a suitable 32.5cm

(13") square of print from a newspaper and, using this as a reference, draw the newsprint onto the board with a black food pen (S.E.p.79). Add pictures by painting with black paste colour diluted in clear spirit.

Cake Preparation

1. Make the paint tin handle and inner rim (S.E.p.23).

2. Level the cakes, stack them using buttercream to secure and place on waxed paper.

3. Colour 170g (6oz) sugarpaste a deep claret colour (a combination of SK Christmas Red and Cyclamen). Spread the top of the cake with buttercream, cover it

with the coloured sugarpaste, then smooth and trim. Press the dry, coloured pastillage ring (S.E.p.23) gently into the sugarpaste to form the upper rim of the tin.

4. Spread buttercream onto the sides of the cake, roll out the remaining white sugarpaste into a long rectangle and cover the cake by wrapping the paste around the sides. Trim the top edge flush with the top of the pastillage ring.

5. Place some softened white sugarpaste and the medium-sized round disc into the sugar shaper and extrude lengths to go around both the inner and outer rims of the top of the paint pot. Stick in position and allow to dry. Then apply a thin coat of Gildesol followed by light gold edible lustre dust.

6. Colour the modelling paste as follows: 90g (3oz) grey, 60g (2oz) black, 140g (5oz) blue and 28g (1oz) yellow. Roll out and cut thin strips of the various colours and stick them to the side of the cake to make the paint pot design. Then, using letter cutters and a food pen, add the written details.

7. Make the lid of the paint tin and a paintbrush (S.E.p.23) and place these, together with the cake, onto the board, securing all in position with sugar glue. Soften the claret-coloured trimmings with water until they have the consistency of thick paint then, with a paintbrush, paint some onto the board. Also add some onto the paintbrush and to the rim of the paint pot, allowing it to run down the sides. Fix the handle to the paint pot with small balls of white sugarpaste and support in position with foam until dry.

8. Glaze all the claret-coloured paint so that it looks wet and shiny.

9. Finally, place a ribbon around the board

SPECIAL *Effects & Accessories*

Paint Tin Handle

Cut a 30cm x 1.5cm (12" x 1/2") strip from thinly rolled pastillage and place on a suitable former. I used a 7" round polystyrene cake dummy. Leave to dry.

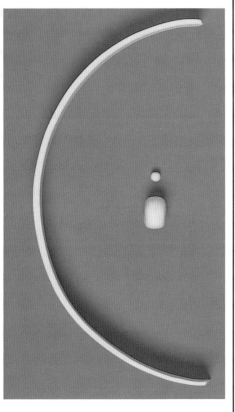

Paint Tin: Inner Top Rim

1. Line the tin originally used to bake the cakes with non-stick, non-absorbent material (e.g. Bake-O-Glide). Roll out the remaining pastillage between 4mm spacers and cut into a 45cm x 2.5cm (18" x 1") strip. Place the strip around the inside of the lined tin and glue the join together to form a ring. Leave to dry thoroughly.

2. Apply Gildesol followed by

light gold edible lustre dust to the inside of the pastillage circle.

Paint Tin Lid

Roll out 225g (8oz) white sugarpaste, then cut a 15cm (6") circle and another fractionally smaller. Glue the smaller circle on top of the larger one. Place some

of the remaining sugarpaste in a sugar shaper together with the medium-sized round disc and extrude a length to fit around the edge of the larger circle. Replace the disc in the sugar shaper, this time with the half circle disc, and extrude enough paste to go around the edge of the smaller circle. Glue the lengths of paste in position and allow to dry. Apply a thin coat of Gildesol over the entire surface of the lid and dust with light gold edible lustre dust.

Paintbrush

1. Roll out some of the pastillage to a thickness of 5mm (3/8") and

cut out the paintbrush using the template (see page 95).
TIP: I find that a small cutting wheel is very good for doing this as it does not drag the paste. Push a wooden dowel through the handle of the brush to make the hole and leave to dry on foam.

2. Colour 85g (3oz) modelling paste black. For the bristles, roll out approximately half of this modelling paste into a fairly thick 5.5cm x 12cm (2 3/8" x 4 3/4") rectangle and attach around the head of the pastillage brush with sugar glue. Then, using the long edge of a small palette knife, cut repeatedly into the paste to give the impression of bristles. For the handle, roll out the remaining black paste and fold it around the handle. Clip the corners, ease in the fullness on the underside and trim off the excess paste.

3. Place a 3cm x 12cm (1 3/8 x 4 3/4") strip of white modelling paste around the middle of the brush, then attach three strips of paste cut with a 2mm strip cutter. Once dry, apply a thin coat Gildesol followed by light silver lustre dust.

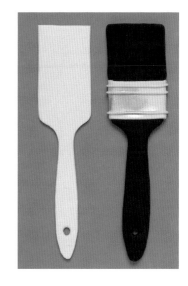

Materials

40.5cm (16") round cake drum
25.5cm (10") round
Madeira cake, Buttercream
(5lb) sugarpaste
60g (2oz) pastillage
Mexican Modelling Paste (MMP),
coloured as follows:
168g (6oz) flesh,28g (1oz) brown
60g (2oz) black
15g (1/2oz) olive green
Flowerpaste to dress the figure:
15g (1/2oz) olive green (SK Holly/Ivy)
60g (2oz) dark brown (SK Bulrush)
15g (1/2oz) black
60g (2oz) dark blue (SK Bluebell)
15g (1/2oz) blue-green
15g (1/2oz) cream
Paste colours: to colour the above
Blues (e.g. Blue bell, Gentian)
Greens (e.g. SK Holly/Ivy, Christmas
Green, Fern) Yellow (SK Daffodil)
Assorted colours for painting the face
Black, White
Dust colours:
Assorted, to colour the reeds (e.g. SK
Shady Moss, Forest Green,
Leaf Green, Vine)
Squires Kitchen Edible Lustre Dusts,
including Silver
Clear spirit, e.g. gin or vodka,
Powdered gelatine, Icing sugar
Small amount of royal icing
Sugar glue,18-gauge wire
Gum tragacanth, Piping gel
Uncooked spaghetti or sugar sticks

Equipment

Stiff-bristled kitchen brush
Dresden tool, Ball tool
Piping tubes: various, including No. 0
2cm (3/4") circle cutter
Medium male template (see page 97)
Holly Products Adult Head Mould
Foam (for drying pastillage and
supporting the figure)
Stitching wheel, Small scissors
Cutting wheel, Scouring pad
Sugar shaper, Paintbrushes
Straight edge, Teaspoon
Small bowl, Cocktail sticks
Waxed or silicone paper
Staysoft or plasticine
20cm (8") plate
Mug, Wire cutters, Ribbon

Ingredients

1/2 teaspoon powered gelatine
1 teaspoon water
1/2 teaspoon icing sugar

FISHING

Fishing or angling is a popular form of recreation worldwide, indeed in many countries it is the most popular of all participant sports. Like hunting, fishing originated as a means of providing food for survival. Although fishing tackle has developed over the years, the basic challenges of fishing remain the same.

Covering the Board

Take 670g (1 1/2lb) sugarpaste and colour portions in various shades of blue, green and brown. Roughly knead these together to produce a marbled effect (S.E.p.69), then cover the water section of the board as shown in Fig.1 and leave to dry.

Carving the Cake

Cut the cake in half and place one half near the top left hand edge of the board as illustrated. Take a sharp knife and shape the cake so that it slopes down towards the water's edge and to where the fisherman will kneel. Slice the second half of the cake horizontally in two and place one half on the uncovered area, cutting it to fit the board. Cut into this cake to make a lower, level area for the path and fishing area. Fill in the area where the fisherman will kneel with some of the remaining cake and, with the rest, add height and shape to the bushes behind the fisherman. TIP: Freeze the cake once you have cut it into three and shape it whilst still frozen.

Fig.1

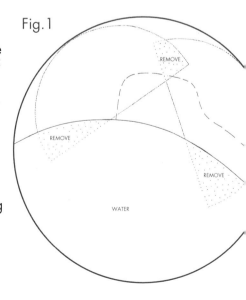

Covering the Cake

This is done in sections, each section being textured before another is covered. Firstly, fill in any holes between the pieces of cake with sugarpaste. Then colour the remaining sugarpaste in various shades of green. Spread a thin layer of buttercream over the path, fishing area and bank and cover with pale green paste. Texture the paste with a stiff bristled kitchen brush (S.E.p.71). Next, cover the shrubs (one at a time) with different coloured green pastes, texturing each before starting the next (S.E.p.71). Once the cake is completely covered, leave to dry. Then, using a combination of diluted green and yellow paste colours, paint over the grass and shrubs (this is optional, but it does bring the cake to life).

Modelling the Fisherman

(For more details on how to make the body parts, please refer to Figure Modelling on pages 92-93.)

1. Using the medium-sized male template (see page 94), model the legs. Bend the left leg into a kneeling position and insert a sugar stick (or length of dried spaghetti) through the thigh to give added support. Shape the right leg into a crouching position, then allow to dry thoroughly.

2. Model the torso and insert spaghetti into the neck and shoulders. Place the kneeling leg in an upright position and secure the torso in place, supporting the figure with foam until the glue has dried. Remove the foam and glue the crouching leg in position. Allow to dry thoroughly.

3. Make the arms and attach them to the body. Position them using foam for support. Close the hands so that they will be able to hold the rod and net: you will find it helpful to place a stick of the same width (e.g. a barbecue skewer) in each hand until dry.

4. Model the head using the medium-sized mould, manipulating it to create a suitable expression. Once the head has dried, add the ears, then paint and dust on the facial details. Place to one side.

5. Dress the fisherman using the suggested flowerpastes (see page 94). Secure the head in position, adjusting the cut of the neck with a craft knife, if necessary. Then make hair from textured strips of dark brown modelling paste (see Figure Modelling section on pages 92-93).

Assembling the Cake

1. Make a fishing tackle box, a fishing rod, the fishing line, some water splashes, a fishing net, some reeds, a discarded boot and a fish (S.E.pp.27-28). Secure the boot in position on the board, place the fish inside and attach the gelatine splashes of water around and to the boot.

2. Glue the fisherman into position, ensuring that he is stable whilst the glue dries. Glue the tackle box in place. Place some softened green sugarpaste trimmings in the sugar shaper together with a mesh disc and extrude clumps of grass (S.E.p.70). Arrange these over the grass areas of the cake.

3. Once the fisherman is secure, place the handle of the net in his left hand. Position the brown half circle of pastillage on the water at the end of the handle, adjusting it so that it is in line; glue in position, supporting it with foam if necessary, and allow to dry. Finish the fishing net (S.E.p.27).

4. Carefully push the reeds through the blue sugarpaste and secure in position with let-down blue sugarpaste.

5. Remove the cocktail sticks from the fishing line and thread one end through the eyelets along the fishing rod. Secure it at the handle with a tiny amount of dark brown flowerpaste. Next, place the rod in the fisherman's right hand (hopefully, this will be a good fit but, as an added precaution, add some extra paste - as well as sugar glue - to secure it). Take the free end of the line and attach it to the boot with a small ball of black paste (glue may dissolve it).

6. Apply piping gel to the board with a paintbrush, using the brush to create ripples.

7. Finally, attach a ribbon around the board.

SPECIAL *Effects & Accessories*

Fishing Net

Place some softened white pastillage in the sugar shaper together with the medium-sized round disc and extrude a 10cm (4") length. Place on foam, straighten and leave to dry. Colour

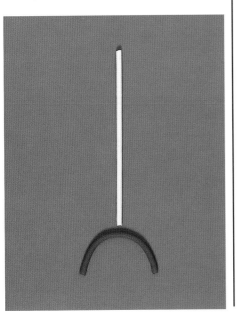

a small amount of pastillage brown and place in the sugar shaper. Extrude a length and position in a curve as shown. Leave to dry. Having positioned these parts in relation to the fisherman (see Assembling the Cake), use a No. 0 piping tube and a small amount of royal icing (to which a tiny amount of gum tragacanth should be added) to hang small loops from the brown pastillage, to form the net. Once dry, paint the net with black paste colour and the handle with silver lustre dust mixed with clear spirit.

Fishing Tackle Box

Take 28g (1oz) of black modelling paste and roll it into a ball. Place a pair of smoothers either side of the ball and squeeze, turn the paste over onto one of the flat sides and squeeze again.

Continue in this fashion until you have an oblong shape with flat sides. Repeat the process with approximately 15g (1/2oz) of olive green modelling paste to make the lid. Once the lid is the same size as the box, glue it in position.

Indent the depression for the handle with a ball tool, then add a black handle and green strips to the top of the box.

Fishing Rod

(To be able to make a fishing rod that was light, strong and thin enough for the fisherman to hold, I had to resort to using a strong wire, so please ensure that the recipient of the cake is aware of this.)

Take an 18-gauge wire and a 20cm (8") plate. Place the plate upside-down on the work surface and bend the wire around the rim to achieve a smooth curve. Place a mug upside-down and curve the top end of the wire to make the top of the rod. Cut off about 2.5cm (1") of the straight piece of wire from this end and 6.5cm (2 1/2") from the other end.

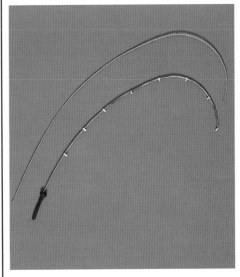

To make the eyelets through which to feed the line, place some softened cream flowerpaste in the sugar shaper together with the small round disc. Extrude small lengths and attach to the wire in loops at 3cm (1 1/4") intervals, so that the loops are at 90 degrees to the rod. Once dry, paint the fishing rod with a mixture of black and white paste colours and blue lustre dust diluted in clear spirit; paint the eyelets with silver lustre dust.

Make the handle from brown flowerpaste as shown in the step; the ball at the top is to help secure the rod in the fisherman's hand. Check that the handle fits snugly in place, then remove and allow to dry.

Reeds

Colour the remaining pastillage in two shades of green and make the reeds (S.E.p.70).

Discarded Boot

Make a 2.5cm (1") ball from black modelling paste, elongate it, then flatten one half to make the front of the foot. Extend the other half upwards to make the ankle. The boot should have a length of 4cm (1^1/$_2$") and be cut to a height of 1.75cm (^{5}/$_8$"). Use a pair of scissors to cut off the toe at an angle so that the boot will look as if it is only partially out of the water. Leave to dry.

Thinly roll out some dark brown flowerpaste and completely cover

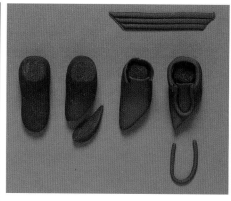

the boot so that the paste joins at the back. Trim the paste to shape around the sole with a small pair of scissors. Cut the paste around the top of the boot 1cm (^{3}/$_8$") higher than the black paste beneath, then cut two slits to form the tongues (see step). Roll a thin sausage of brown paste and place on the front of the boot as illustrated. Make the ankle support from a strip of paste, indent with a straight edge and stick around the top of the boot. Finish this off with a further sausage of brown paste placed around the top of the boot.

Fish

To make the fish, take a small amount of white modelling paste and model the fish's head. Use a small pair of scissors to cut into the paste to make the mouth and open it up slightly with a Dresden tool. Once dry, cut the fish to size. Dilute some lustre dust colours in clear spirit and paint the fish. Finally, dilute some black, yellow and green paste colours and paint the eye and other markings, then leave to dry.

Fishing Line & Water Splashes

Place the ingredients listed on page 24 in a small bowl and allow the gelatine to absorb the water. Heat the bowl gently over a pan of simmering water until the gelatine has dissolved. Use a teaspoon to pour small amounts of the mixture onto waxed (or silicone) paper, encouraging the liquid to form irregular shapes to represent splashes. To make the fishing line, continue heating the mixture until it starts to form a skin. Remove it from the heat, then place a cocktail stick on the edge of the skin and slowly and gently pull out a thread. Once you have pulled out a long thread, take another cocktail stick and place it at the bowl end of the tread: you should now be able to remove the thread from the bowl. Place the cocktail sticks in florist's staysoft or plasticine to allow the thread to dry.

Whilst the gelatine is still rubbery, peel the splashes from their paper and arrange them in more interesting shapes. Leave to go crisp: you will find that they curve even more as they dry.

MORE SPECIAL
Effects

Waves

In order to give the waves some height, place sausages of blue sugarpaste on the board at right angles to the direction in which the waves are travelling. Shape these sausages by hand so that the paste is high at the front of the wave and slopes downwards at the back (see photograph). Marble some blue sugarpaste and cover the waves; smooth it into position. Once dry, add the surf by placing some white royal icing or let-down white sugarpaste on a paintbrush and applying it to the tips of the waves. Once this is dry, cover all the water and surf with piping gel so that the water becomes reflective and the colours intensify.

Dew/Raindrops

You can achieve this effect using either piping gel or gelatine. In my opinion, piping gel gives the most realistic results and is by far the quickest method, but if you are melting gelatine to make, say, some water splashes, why not have a go at a few dew/rain drops at the same time, particularly as they will keep for future use.

Using Gelatine

Prepare the gelatine as for the water splashes. Secure a piece of cellophane or waxed paper to a flat surface with masking tape. Dip a paintbrush or cocktail stick into the gelatine solution and place a drop onto the prepared surface. Allow this to set for several hours until hard, then attach it to the sugar work or store in an airtight container until required.

Using Piping Gel

(NOTE: If placing gel on a painted or dusted surface such as a leaf, remember to steam or varnish it first to set the dust, otherwise the gel may affect the colour.)

Dip a fine paintbrush (or a cocktail stick) into the pot of piping gel, then carefully touch the surface upon which the droplet is to appear with the tip of the brush or stick. If you wish to make hanging droplets, strengthen the gel by softening it gently. To do this, place a teaspoon of gel in a small container and place this in a bowl of hot water until the gel has softened but before it turns to liquid, then continue as before.

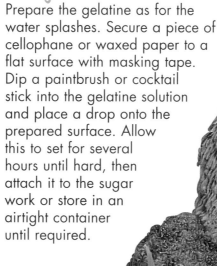

29

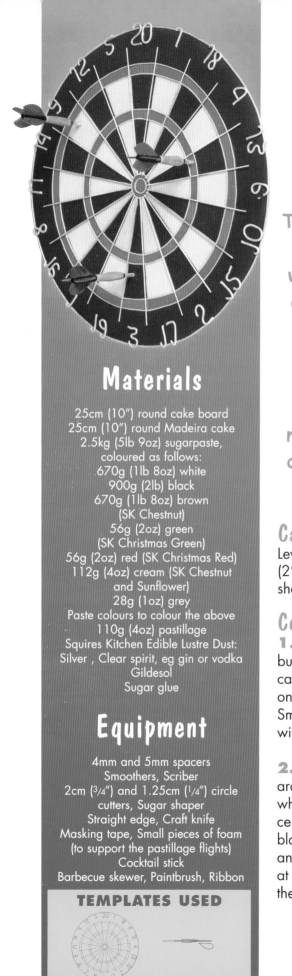

Materials

25cm (10") round cake board
25cm (10") round Madeira cake
2.5kg (5lb 9oz) sugarpaste,
coloured as follows:
670g (1lb 8oz) white
900g (2lb) black
670g (1lb 8oz) brown
(SK Chestnut)
56g (2oz) green
(SK Christmas Green)
56g (2oz) red (SK Christmas Red)
112g (4oz) cream (SK Chestnut
and Sunflower)
28g (1oz) grey
Paste colours to colour the above
110g (4oz) pastillage
Squires Kitchen Edible Lustre Dust:
Silver , Clear spirit, eg gin or vodka
Gildesol
Sugar glue

Equipment

4mm and 5mm spacers
Smoothers, Scriber
2cm (3/4") and 1.25cm (1/4") circle
cutters, Sugar shaper
Straight edge, Craft knife
Masking tape, Small pieces of foam
(to support the pastillage flights)
Cocktail stick
Barbecue skewer, Paintbrush, Ribbon

TEMPLATES USED

Darts

The modern game of darts can be traced back to Roman and Greek times when weighted arrows were thrown in warfare. Popular ever since, it is even believed that the Pilgrim Fathers played a form of darts as a pastime on board the Mayflower as they made their way to the New World in 1620. The game has been known as a sport in its present form since 1896, when the numbering system was devised. In Britain today, darts remains a very popular form of recreation in many pubs and social clubs.

Cake Preparation

Level the cake to a height of 5cm (2") and attach to the board. It should fit exactly.

Covering the dartboard

1. Spread a thin layer of buttercream over the top of the cake and cover the top surface only with white sugarpaste. Smooth, then cut the edges flush with the sides.

2. Brush cooled boiled water around the outside edge of the white sugarpaste, leaving the centre dry in order that sections of black paste can easily be removed and replaced by coloured sections at a later stage. Cover the sides of the cake with buttercream. Place the cake on top of a smaller board to lift it off the work surface. Then roll out the black sugarpaste between 4mm spacers and cover the cake bringing the paste down over the board and trimming the edges flush with the base of the board. Carefully smooth and leave to dry.

3. Using the dartboard template (see page 97) and a scriber, transfer the dartboard pattern onto the top of the cake, making sure it is positioned centrally.

4. The dartboard is constructed by removing one piece of sugarpaste and replacing it with another of a different colour. Start in the centre of the dartboard and,

31

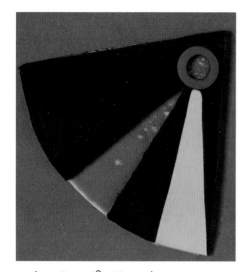

turned grey). Roll out a small amount of green paste between 5mm spacers, cut a 2cm (3/4") circle and place in this central hole. Smooth to fit. Then, using the 1.25cm (1/4") circle cutter, cut out the small central circle from the green paste and replace with a

red bullseye circle (made in the same way as the green circle).

5. Using a straight edge and a craft knife, cut along all the scribed radial lines of the dartboard, then cut around the outer edge of the scoring area. Remove the black triangle to the right of the top triangle and replace it with pale brown paste that has been rolled between 4mm spacers and cut out using the template. Smooth and adjust as necessary (it does not have to fit the outside edge exactly as the doubles ring will replace this area at a later stage). Repeat

with a 2cm (3/4") circle cutter, cut the larger central circle from the black paste and remove to reveal the white paste below (it may have

this procedure for all the alternate triangles.

6. Cut out the triples ring (the middle ring) with a craft knife, then glue short 4mm deep strips of red and green paste into place around the ring, as appropriate. Repeat for the doubles ring.

7. Take the fine mesh disc of a sugar shaper and cover all but one hole with masking tape. Place the disc in the shaper with the taped side facing inwards. Soften the light grey sugarpaste, place it in the sugar shaper and extrude some of the paste, placing it around the outside edges of the double, triple and bullseye circles. Allow to dry.

8. Replace the mesh disc with the smallest round disc and extrude some more grey paste, this time placing it around the top of the upper edge of the cake to form the band for the numbers. Allow to dry.

9. Paint all the grey paste with silver lustre dust diluted in clear spirit.

10. Make holes in the dartboard with a cocktail stick to represent the marks of previous games.

Pastillage Pieces

1. Place the mesh disc (as used in Point 7 above) and some softened white pastillage in a sugar shaper and extrude 20, 10cm (4") lengths. Straighten each length and allow to dry. (You will also need pastillage lengths for the darts, see below.)

2. Replace the mesh disc with the small round disc and extrude approximately 2.5cm (1") of pastillage. Use it to shape one of the numbers and repeat until all the numbers are complete. Allow to dry.

3. When dry, apply Gildesol and silver lustre dust to the 10cm (4") lengths and to the numbers.

Assembling the Cake

Carefully attach the numbers around the number ring and the lengths in a radial pattern over the joins between the light brown and black paste. Finally make and attach the darts. (see below)

SPECIAL *Effects* & *Accessories*

The Darts

1. Place the medium-sized round disc in the sugar shaper and extrude three 10cm (4") lengths; straighten and leave to dry. Using the dart template (see page 97) make 12 flights from thinly rolled pastillage and leave to dry, turning them over from time to time.

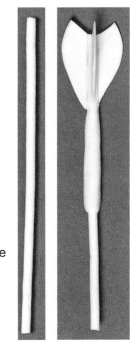

2. Using the template as a guide, build up the body of the dart with sugarpaste. Once dry, attach the flights with a thick sugar glue made from pastillage. Support each flight with pieces of foam until the glue has dried completely.

3. Decorate the darts using paste colours diluted in spirit and edible lustre dusts.

4. Once dry, make holes for the darts in the cake with a barbecue skewer. Place thick sugar glue in each hole, then position the darts.
NOTE: Remember that pastillage, although strong, is very brittle, so do be careful not to knock the darts off the board.

33

Materials

30.5cm x 23cm (12" x 9")
oblong cake drum
3 x 10cm (4") round Madeira cakes
and a 12.5cm (5") square cake
(alternatively, bake 3 larger cakes
and cut to size
Buttercream
Sugarpaste:
500g (1lb 2oz) black
1kg (2lb 4oz) white
112g (4oz) cream
28g (1oz) pastillage
225g (8oz) white Mexican
Modelling Paste (MMP)
Flowerpaste:, 28g (1oz) blue
60g (2oz) white
Paste colours:
brown (SK Chestnut and
Teddy Bear Brown)
orange (SK Berberis)
blue (SK Gentian)
White (SK Edelweiss)
Squires Kitchen Edible Lustre Dusts:
Silver and Burnt Copper
Clear spirit, e.g. gin or vodka
Gildesol, Sugar glue

Equipment

Crown cork (bottle top)
Material to make mould, e.g. Ann
Baber's Moulding Gel or Silicone
Plastique
Small palette knife, Dresden tool
Paintbrushes (including a large
flat-headed one), Teaspoon
Cutting wheel, Smoother
Waxed paper, Bag of sugar (for
reference), Flat piece of foam
Craft knife, Spacers,
Letter cutters, Dowel
Food pens:
blue (SK Gentian and Bluebell)
black (SK Blackberry)
red (SK Poinsettia)

TEMPLATES USED

Home Brewing

Beer, which can be made from a number of high starch cereal grains, has always been a popular drink, as it stores very well and is adaptable to all climates. Records show that beer was brewed from barley in Sumeria and Babylonia as long ago as 6000BC. It is also depicted on reliefs in Egyptian tombs dating from 2400BC. The basic techniques of brewing came to Europe from the Middle East. At first, beer was brewed at home and in monasteries then by the late Middle Ages it had become a commercial product. Brewing was a winter occupation until ice making and refrigeration equipment was developed in the late 19th century.

Today, beer is a large scale manufacturing industry in almost all industrialised countries. However, some enthusiasts prefer to brew their own, a hobby that has increased in popularity since the introduction of home brew kits such as the one depicted here.

Covering the Board

Take 670g (1^1/$_2$lb) white sugarpaste and cover the board. Once it has dried, dilute some brown paste colour (SK Teddy Bear Brown) in clear spirit and paint in sweeping strokes with a large flat-headed brush.

Carving the Cakes

1. Level the cakes. If you have baked cakes larger than the 10cm (4") ones required, make a 10cm (4") circle template and use it to cut the cakes to size. Spread a thin layer of buttercream over the top of two of the cakes, then stack all three cakes. Cut the stacked cakes to an overall height of 19cm (7^1/$_2$") and place on waxed paper.

2. Cut the square cake to make a shape approximately 13cm (5") high, 9cm (3^1/$_2$") wide and 6cm (2^3/$_8$") deep; alternatively, use the cake trimmings from the larger cakes to make this shape. Then have a look at a bag of sugar and adjust the shape of the cake as you think appropriate. Place on waxed paper.

Covering the Bag of Sugar Cake

1. Spread a thin layer of buttercream over the cake. Roll out

34

the remaining white sugarpaste into a rectangle long enough to wrap around the cake and high enough

to fold over on the top. Starting at the back, carefully wrap the paste around the cake and rub the join until it disappears. Fold the paste over on the top of the cake so that it resembles the folds on a bag of sugar. Then use a Dresden tool to mark irregular creases on the bag and allow to dry.

2. To make it easier to decorate the bag of sugar, lie the back of the bag carefully on some foam so that the front of the bag is uppermost. Use a scriber to mark the large and small rectangles on the front and sides of the bag. Dilute some orange paste colour (SK Berberis) in clear spirit and apply a wash to the paste inside each rectangle. Once dry, transfer your chosen words to the sugar packet using the template (see page 97) and a scriber, then add colour using food pens. There is plenty of scope here to personalise the cake.

Covering the Home Brew Kit Cake

1. Measure the circumference of the cake, then cover the sides with a thin layer of buttercream. Roll out the black sugarpaste between spacers and cut it into a rectangle the length of the circumference and the height of the cake. Carefully roll up the paste and then, starting at the back, unroll it around the cake. Smooth the join closed. Next, roll out some more black paste and cut a circle with the same diameter as the cake top. Stick in position with buttercream. Smooth the sides and top of the cake with smoothers.

2. Place the oval template (see page 97) on the front of the cake and cut around it with a craft knife. Roll out the cream sugarpaste between spacers and, using the template cut out an oval shape. Remove the black oval of sugarpaste from the cake and replace it with the cream one.

3. Cut out a 10cm (4") x 11.5cm (4¹/₂") rectangle from the back of the cake and replace it with a white one of the same size.

4. Once the paste has hardened, transfer the chosen design to the cream oval. As for the sugar packet, you will probably find it easier to place the cake on foam to support it in a horizontal position. Draw the background with a black food pen, then paint the beer in the glass using a selection of brown and orange paste colours diluted in clear spirit.

5. The white rectangle at the rear of the can is a label giving

instructions for use and a barcode: write these on with a black food pen.

6. Thinly roll out the blue flowerpaste, cut a 4.5cm x 6cm (1³/₄" x 2³/₈") rectangle and stick in position on the front of the can. Once dry, write on your chosen words with a food pen.

7. Decide on the name of the beer, then cut out the appropriate letters from white flowerpaste using letter cutters. Again, there are lots of possibilities here for personalising the cake.

8. To make the lid, roll out some of the remaining black sugarpaste between spacers and cut a 3cm (1¹/₄") wide strip. Glue this strip to the top of the tin then, with a dowel

held vertically, press into the paste at regular intervals. Adjust the edges using a smoother and a craft knife.

Assembling the Cake

Make the crown corks, a teaspoon and a paddle (S.E.p.37). Place the cakes and accessories in position on the board and, once you are happy with the arrangement, secure in position. Use a craft knife to shorten the handle of the paddle where it comes off the board and conceal the join in the handle with a small sausage of white paste.

SPECIAL *Effects* & *Accessories*

Crown Corks

Make a mould from the topside of a crown cork: I used moulding gel to make mine. Place some of the white modelling

paste into the mould and cut it

level with a small palette knife. Release the paste from the mould and tidy the edges, if necessary, with a Dresden tool. Once dry, mix some silver lustre dust with clear spirit and paint around the fluted edges of the cork. Then mix some burnt copper lustre dust in the same way and paint the tops of the corks. You will probably need to apply two coats. To make the dark corks, dilute some blue (SK Gentian) paste colour and apply it over the top of the copper: again, you will need to use two coats.

Teaspoon

Roll out the pastillage on a lightly greased board and press the teaspoon into the icing to indent the shape. Cut around the outline with a cutting wheel, then place on the spoon to dry. Use a paintbrush to apply a layer of Gildesol over the spoon, then brush on the silver lustre dust.

Paddle

Roll out the white modelling paste to an overall thickness of 8mm ($^3/_8$"). Place the template (see page 97) on the paste as a guide, then gradually reduce the thickness of the paste so that the majority of the paddle has a thickness of 2mm ($^1/_8$"). Cut out the paddle with a cutting wheel and place to one side to dry. Using a smoother, roll out the remaining modelling paste into a 1.5cm ($^5/_8$") wide sausage and place on the end of the paddle. (NOTE: Do not stick at this stage.)

MORE SPECIAL *Effects*

METALLIC EFFECTS

Now that edible metallic colours are available, it is possible to create all sorts of metallic effects on cakes. Throughout this book, I have used the Squires Kitchen Dust Colour range and have found that the way to apply the dust depends very much on the size of the object to be covered.

For large objects, e.g. the spanner shown, the best way to apply an

even coat of silver is first of all to cover the object lightly with Gildesol and then to dust the silver over the top with a brush. For small objects, such as the trimmings on the car and dartboard, mix the dust with clear spirit and use it as paint: you will probably need to apply two coats.

Silver Foil

Thinly roll out some white flowerpaste and place over some scrunched up foil (see step), ensuring it is pushed well into all the creases. Once dry, remove and apply Gildesol and silver dust.

Materials

40.5cm x 35.5cm (16" x 14")
oval cake drum
25.5cm (10") round Madeira cake
Buttercream
308g (11 oz) Mexican Modelling
Paste (MMP):
168g (6oz) flesh
112g (4oz) white
28g (1oz) brown
2.13kg (4lb 12oz) sugarpaste,
coloured as follows:
450g (1lb) white
1.568kg (3½lb) green
112g (4oz) sand
60g (2oz) soft brown sugar
(unrefined light muscovado)
15g (½oz) pastillage
Paste colours:
White (SK Edelweiss), Black
Greens (e.g. SK Fern, Vine,
Christmas Green and Holly/Ivy)
Yellow (SK Daffodil)
Squires Kitchen Edible Lustre Dust:
Silver
Clear spirit, e.g. gin or vodka
Flowerpaste:
28g (1oz) red (SK Poinsettia)
28g (1oz) dark blue (SK Bluebell)
28g (1oz) cream,15g (½oz) black
Sugar sticks (or spaghetti)
Sugar glue

Equipment

Stiff-bristled kitchen brush (for
texturing the grass)
Smoother, Ribbon
Straight edge, e.g. ruler
Medium male template
(see page 97)
Holly Products Adult Head Mould
Mini stitching wheel
Small scissors, Cutting wheel
Paintbrushes, Sugar shaper
Tweezers, Foam (for drying
pastillage and supporting the figure)
Wooden dowel, No. 2 piping tube
Food pen: dark red (SK Cyclamen)

Golf

The earliest recorded reference to golf is an Act of the Scottish Parliament dated 1457, in which James II of Scotland bans the game in order to encourage his subjects to concentrate on archery in an effort to drive out the English. Although the origins of golf are uncertain, it is generally accepted that the game was devised and developed on the links of the East Coast of Scotland. There golf was played for nearly 400 years before expanding west and south with the advent of the railways. Golf was then taken further afield by empire builders and traders to places like India, China and America. But it was in America that the game took hold and where the greatest influence over its development has taken place. More recently, television has greatly popularised the sport and has encouraged sponsorship, making golf the multi-million pound business that it is today.

Carving the Cake

Level the cake to a height of 5cm (2") and place it to the back of the board as illustrated in Fig.1. Cut the remaining cake into pieces and place the pieces in the shaded area, thereby enlarging the putting green and disguising the edge of the cake. To add more visual interest, place the pieces at varying heights; then, when you are happy with the arrangement, secure them in position with buttercream. Fill any holes between the cake pieces with white sugarpaste.

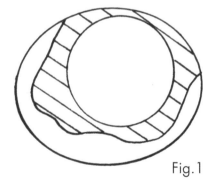

Fig.1

Covering the Cake

Cover the area of the bunker with sand-coloured sugarpaste, securing it in position with buttercream. Then spread

38

39

buttercream over the remainder of the cake and cover with the green sugarpaste. Cut out the bunker to reveal the sand-coloured paste beneath. Next, texture the grass with a clean, dry kitchen brush or bottle brush (S.E.p.71). Take a smoother and flatten the putting green to resemble closely cut grass (I have used artistic licence here, making the green smaller than it would actually be.) Once dry, paint the grass with various diluted green and yellow paste colours, making the putting green lighter than the rough grass. When this has dried, brush sugar glue over the bunker and sprinkle with soft brown sugar to resemble sand. Then rake the sugar: I actually did this with a small toy rake, but any pointed tool will do the job.

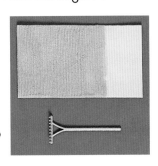

Modelling the Golfer

(For more details on how to make the body parts, please refer to Figure Modelling on pages 92-93.)

1. Legs: Using the medium-sized male template (see page 94), model the legs, cutting them straight at crotch level rather than at an angle (see photograph). Bend the legs into a kneeling position, then insert sugar sticks or lengths of dried spaghetti through

the thighs to give added support. Allow the legs to dry thoroughly, supporting them in an upright kneeling position.

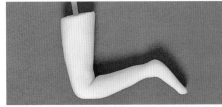

2. Torso: Model the torso, again cutting it straight at crotch level, shape the buttocks and bend the neck. Insert spaghetti into the neck and shoulders. Glue the torso to the top of the legs and position the back, supporting it on foam. Allow to dry thoroughly.

3. Arms: Make the arms and attach to the body. Position them under the body as in the main photo, keeping the foam under the body so that the arms maintain their shape whilst they dry. Allow to dry thoroughly before dressing the figure, so as to prevent any limbs from falling off.

4. Head: Model the head using the medium-sized mould and manipulate it so that it looks as though the golfer might be trying to blow the ball into the hole. Once dry, add his ears, then paint and dust the facial detail. Place to one side.

Dressing the Golfer

Dress the golfer (S.E.p.94) using the suggested flowerpastes and decorate the trouser fabric as opposite. Secure the head in position, adjusting the cut of the

neck with a craft knife, before making the collar. Next make and attach the hair (see Figure Modelling on pages 93).

Assembling the Cake

Make a golf bag, golf clubs, and a flag (S.E.pp.40-41). Attached the golf bag to the cake, half fill the top of the bag with some sugarpaste trimmings that have been coloured black. Then, using tweezers, arrange the golf clubs in the bag, with the exception of the putter, by carefully pushing them through the black paste. Finally, make and attach the two carrying straps from strips of flowerpaste. Decide on the position of the golfer and glue him in place. To make the hole, insert a wooden dowel carefully through the putting green and remove. Paint the inside of the hole with neat white paste colour. Next, make the ball from cream flowerpaste and place it on the edge of the hole. Place the putter to the right of the golfer (or to his left if he is left-handed). Finally, attach the ribbon around the board.

SPECIAL *Effects & Accessories*

Golf Bag

With a smoother, roll a cylinder of white modelling paste 2.5cm (1") wide and 8cm (3$\frac{1}{4}$") long. Next, roll a cylinder 1.5cm x 7cm (2 $\frac{3}{4}$"), slice through the top at an angle (see step) and attach it to the side of the bag with sugar glue. Then mould the small pocket from a 2cm ($\frac{3}{4}$") ball of modelling paste and attach it to the opposite side of the bag. Allow to dry. Fill the joins between

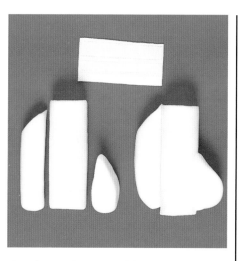

the three shapes with more paste to give the bag a smooth appearance.

Start covering the bag by thinly rolling out some cream flowerpaste and cutting a strip to fit over the large pocket on the side of the bag. Glue in place then, with a mini stitching wheel, make lines of stitches to represent the seams in the fabric. Next, cut two triangles of cream paste and place them either side of this strip. Continue in this fashion, adding additional strips and stitching lines as desired and using the photograph as a guide. Extend the height of the golf bag by 1cm ($^3/_8$") with a strip of blue flowerpaste and leave to dry in an upright position.

Golf Clubs

To make the golf clubs, place some softened pastillage and the small round disc in a sugar shaper and extrude a number of lengths. Place these on foam, straighten and leave to dry. (TIP: Make the flagpole whilst you have the pastillage in the sugar shaper - see The Flag for instructions.) Make a small ball from cream flowerpaste, pinch it into the shape of a club and glue to the end of a pastillage length. Repeat for the other clubs. Make the putter from a 10cm (4") length of pastillage. Once dry, paint the clubs with silver lustre dust mixed with clear spirit. On the putter wrap a 4cm (1$^1/_2$") strip of blue flowerpaste around the top of the shaft to make the handle.

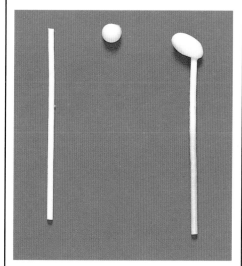

The Flag

Place some pastillage and the medium-sized round disc in the sugar shaper and extrude a length of 18cm (7"). Place it onto foam and straighten. Once dry, paint the 2cm ($^3/_4$") wide black bands with paste colour and, once this is dry, position it on the cake. Cut a flag from thinly rolled red flowerpaste and attach it to the end of the flagpole.

Fabrics

Thinly roll out some flowerpaste in the colour of your choice and, if appropriate, cut it into the relevant shape. Use food pens to draw on the desired pattern, using a straight edge where necessary. The fabric may then be used to clothe a figure.

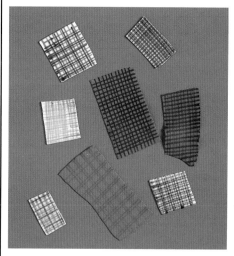

MORE SPECIAL Effects

For fabric where some relaxation of shape is desired, place scrunched up cling film (or similar) under the relevant area to lend a sense of movement to the fabric. Remove the cling film once the flowerpaste is dry.

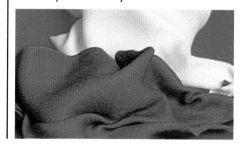

Materials

40.5cm x 35.5cm (16"x 14")
oval cake drum
2 x 18cm (7") round
Madeira cakes
Buttercream
2kg(4lb 8oz) sugarpaste
1.24kg (2lb 12oz)
Mexican Modelling
Paste (MMP):
112g (4oz) orange
450g (1lb) pale green
450g (1lb) cream
168g (6oz) white
56g (2oz) black
Paste colours to colour
the above plus:
Green (SK Holly/Ivy)
Yellow (SK Sunflower)
Brown (SK Chestnut)
Red liquid colour
(SK Poinsettia)
Dusts: Brown (SK Chestnut)
Cream (SK Desert Storm)
Green (SK Holly/Ivy)
Orange (SK Marigold)
Squires Kitchen Edible Lustre
Dust: Silver
112g (4oz) pastillage
Gildesol
Trex or White Flora
Clear spirit, Sugar glue

Equipment

Serrated kitchen knife
Sugar shaper
Paintbrushes
3cm (1¼") circle cutter
Food pen
Cutting wheel
Dresden tool
Ball tool
Smoother
Number cutters

Cooking
Birthday Hotpot!

The art of cooking dates back to the time when primitive man first used fire to cook his food. One of the earliest fully developed cuisines was that of the ancient Chinese, whose references date back to the 5th century BC.

Another early centre noted for its sophisticated cuisine was Rome. The mid-15th century invention of the printing press was responsible for major changes in the culinary arts, as it made cookery books much more widely available. An Italian produced the first known cookery book in 1485: it contained recipes for marzipans and other sweets. In the 20th century, refrigeration, air transport and modern food processing have had a huge impact by greatly increasing the variety of food available.

Today there is great interest in food, with many ingredients and dishes being prepared and eaten that 50 years ago were unheard of outside their country of origin. I enjoy cooking and experimenting with new recipes and so have created this cake for those of you with a similar passion for cooking good food.

Covering the Board

1. Colour 1.12kg (2lb 8oz) of sugarpaste pale brown. Place the oval cake drum on top of a smaller board to lift it off the work surface, then cover the oval board, bringing the sugarpaste over the sides. Cut away the excess and partially allow it to dry. Then, with a kitchen knife, repeatedly cut into the paste in different directions to represent knife scores on the chopping board.

2. Paint the board to look like wood with brown paste colour diluted in clear spirit (S.E.p.54). The knife scores will now look like old cuts, as they will have taken up the brown paste colour. To make more recent marks repeatedly cut the paste again: this time the cuts will remain light in colour.

Carving the Cake

Level both cakes and sandwich them together with buttercream. With a sharp knife curve the base of the cake and carefully carve the top so that the dish has a slightly domed lid (see Fig.1).

42

43

Fig.1

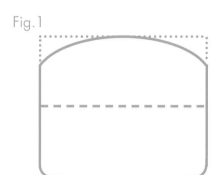

Covering the Cake

1. Place the cake on waxed paper and cover it with a thin layer of buttercream. Take approximately 225g (1lb) of white sugarpaste, roll out a circle and cover the top of the cake to make the lid of the casserole. Carefully cut the paste to shape and smooth the edge so that it blends with side of the cake.

2. Roll out the remaining white sugarpaste into a 12cm x 54cm (4¾" x 21¼") rectangle. Wrap this around the sides of the cake, placing one of the long edges around the top of the casserole dish and tucking the other under the base. Smooth the join and allow to dry.

3. Place some white sugarpaste into a sugar shaper together with the half circle disc, extrude a suitable length and stick it onto the cake to form the rim of the lid.

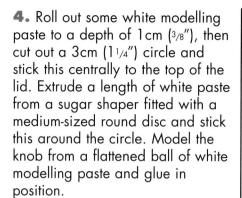

4. Roll out some white modelling paste to a depth of 1cm (³/₈"), then cut out a 3cm (1¼") circle and stick this centrally to the top of the lid. Extrude a length of white paste from a sugar shaper fitted with a medium-sized round disc and stick this around the circle. Model the knob from a flattened ball of white modelling paste and glue in position.

5. To make the handles, roll a 1.75cm (⁵/₈") thick sausage of white modelling paste and cut off the ends. Then cut the resulting cylinder in half and squeeze the cut ends between fingers. Bend slightly and stick to either side of the casserole.

6. Once the paste has dried, take a natural sponge and some liquid red colour or diluted paste colour and sponge paint the casserole dish. Once this has dried, mix up some very dilute brown and sponge paint this over the red. You will find that this tones down the red slightly.

Assembling the Cake

Make an old recipe card, a knife and vegetables (S.E.pp.44-45). Arrange these components and the cake on the chopping board and, once you are happy with the overall effect, secure in position. Then, with a soft paintbrush, brush a little Trex or White Flora over the cut surfaces of the vegetables to make them glisten. Finally, smooth a little White Flora onto the surface of the casserole dish for a glazed look.

SPECIAL *Effects* & *Accessories*

Old Recipe Card

Thinly roll out the pastillage and cut a 9cm x 15cm (3½" x 6") rectangle. I decided to make my recipe card an old and much loved one, looking slightly tatty and yellowed with

age. To do this, place some pieces of waxed paper or cling film under the edges of the card whilst it dries. Once thoroughly dry, dust with yellow/brown dusts (SK Flesh and Chestnut) then, holding the card carefully, pass it through the steam of a kettle to set the dusts. Once dry, write the recipe with a food pen.

Knife

Thinly roll out the remaining pastillage, then press the serrations of a large kitchen knife into the paste. With a cutting wheel cut around the serrated impression, then take a smaller kitchen knife and use this as a template to cut out the remainder of the knife shape. Allow to dry. Model the knife's handle from black modelling paste and stick in position. Attach small balls of white paste on the handle as rivets. Once dry, apply Gildesol to the knife blade and rivets, then dust with edible silver lustre dust.

44

Vegetables

You will find that having real vegetables to study in front of you will make modelling them a lot easier.

1. Carrots: Model three carrots from orange modelling paste. Press the larger end of a ball tool into the carrot tops, then press a cutting wheel into the sides to make a series of marks as illustrated; allow to dry. Add some white paste to the remaining orange modelling paste. Use this to make some thin lengths to stick into the cuts in the carrots, flattening into place with a

Dresden tool. Place small balls of the lighter orange paste in the holes in the carrot tops and texture with the pointed end of a Dresden tool. For the taproots, roll thin tapered lengths of paste and stick in place. Dust the carrot with orange dusts if desired.

2. Courgettes: Model courgettes from pale green modelling paste. Take a smoother and rub it along the length to produce a slightly flattened area; repeat until you have a number of these running along the lengths of all the courgettes. Allow the paste to harden. Dilute some dark green paste colour in clear spirit and paint the courgettes. To make the skin markings, use the sharper end of a Dresden tool and remove some of the colour, as illustrated, to reveal the pale green paste underneath. To make the stalk, roll a suitably sized sausage of modelling paste, cut off one end

then ,with a Dresden tool, press and drag the paste to make ridges. Stick in position and, once dry, paint as the courgette. Stick small circles of cream modelling paste to the flower ends of the courgettes, texture with the shaper end of a Dresden tool and dust with brown. Partially slice up one of the courgettes, then paint and dust the slices as illustrated.

3. Potatoes: Model the potatoes from cream modelling paste: again, use a real vegetable for reference. With

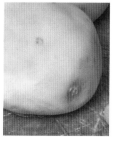

the smaller end of a ball tool, make small impressions for the potatoes' eyes. Once the potatoes have hardened, place small pieces of paste in these indents. Slice up one of the potatoes with a sharp knife and use number cutters to make potato numbers. Paint the potatoes' eyes with diluted brown paste colour and add some other additional marks. Then dust the potatoes with a light yellow-brown (SK Sand Storm) to colour their skins.

MORE SPECIAL Effects

Fruit

1. Apple: The best way to achieve a realistic apple shape is to have one in front of you. Model the apple from pale green modelling paste and allow to dry.

Again using an apple for reference, paint on the prominent markings using paste colours diluted in clear spirit. Once these are dry, dust on the more subtle shading.

2. Orange: Model the orange from modelling paste and texture the surface using a scouring pad. Once firm, paint over the textured surface with diluted orange paste colour to bring out the texturing

and allow to dry. Add the shiny waxed surface by brushing the orange with White Flora or Trex.

3. Bananas: Using a real one as a guide, model a banana from yellow modelling paste and, once dry, paint the markings onto the skin and stalk with diluted brown and black paste colours. Add any green areas with green dust once the paste colours are dry.

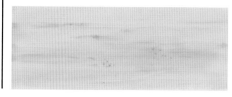

Materials

35cm x 30cm (14" x 12") oval board
20cm (8") round Madeira cake
Buttercream
60g (2oz) pastillage
1.2kg (2lb 11oz) sugarpaste
280g (10oz) Mexican Modelling Paste (MMP):
15g (1/2oz) black, 225g (8oz) flesh, 15g (1/2oz) grey
25g (1oz) orange
84g (3oz) flowerpaste:
green (various shades)
dark blue (SK Bluebell)
light blue (SK Bluebell with White)
yellow (SK Daffodil with a touch of Marigold)
Paste colours:
brown (SK Chestnut)
black (SK Blackberry)
yellow (SK Sunflower)
green (SK Mint)
Assorted colours for painting the bike
Dust colours:
browns (SK Bulrush, Chestnut, Desert Storm and Etruscan Brick), greens (SK Cactus, Green Envy, Leaf Green, Lichen Glow and Shady Moss)
orange (SK Berberis)
Small amount of royal icing
Dowel/sugar stick
Clear spirit, e.g. gin or vodka
Sugar glue

Equipment

28-gauge white wires
Dresden tool, Kitchen grater
Pestle and mortar, Leaf cutters, e.g. fern, Wire cutters
Pliers, Sugar shaper
Piping tube: No. 0
Ball tool, Cutting wheel
Holly Products Adult Head Mould, Paintbrushes, Foam (for supporting the pastillage pieces), Food pen

TEMPLATE USED

Mountain Biking

Mountain biking is reputed to be one of the fastest growing outdoor activities in the world. It appeals to a wide variety of people as it can be either a demanding or a relaxing way of enjoying the countryside.

Carving the Cake

Cut the cake into a crescent shape as illustrated in Fig.1 and place it on the left-hand side of the board. Randomly cut up the remaining cake and place the pieces on top of and around the sides of the crescent so that the cake resembles a rocky outcrop. Once you are happy with the arrangement and have ensured that you have left enough space for the bike trail on the right, secure all the pieces with buttercream.

Fig.1

Covering the Cake

1. Colour 1.12kg (2lb 8oz) sugarpaste in a range of warm greys (I used five different shades).

Roughly mix these together to make a marbled paste (S.E.p.69). Spread a thin layer of buttercream over the cake, then cover both cake and board with the marbled sugarpaste. Texture the rocks with a Dresden tool (S.E.p.49).

You may find it easier to cover the cake in sections rather than as a whole because of the irregular shape of the cake. To do this, spread buttercream over the area you plan to cover, then place a suitably sized piece of sugarpaste on top. Continue with other pieces, smoothing the joins or incorporating them into the rock design, until the cake and board are completely covered.

2. Once the sugarpaste has hardened, colour the

46

47

rocks with a selection of dusts. I have used browns and greens to represent a mossy, damp environment.

3. Prepare some soil (S.E.p.59) and glue in position. Then make roots and vegetation for added detail:

Roots: To make the plant roots, add brown paste colour to some of the grey sugarpaste trimmings. Then, using the medium-sized holes of a

kitchen grater, grate the brown paste. You will find that this gives irregular strands of paste, ideal for the representation of entangled roots. Brush sugar glue over the areas of rock where the plants will grow, then separate a few strands of paste at a time and secure them in position.

Vegetation:
Make a selection of plants using flowerpaste in various shades of green and a

variety of cutters. Make some tufts of grass (S.E.p.70) and secure in position.

THE BIKE
The Wheels
Make two wheels for the mountain bike (S.E.p.49).

The Frame
The frame is made from lengths of dried pastillage, snapped to the correct length and stuck together.

1. Place some white pastillage and the medium-sized round disc in the sugar shaper and extrude

some straight lengths. Pick up one of these lengths and place over the template of the front forks (see page 97).

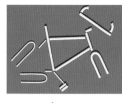

Allow all the pieces to dry.

2. Replace the disc in the sugar shaper with the small round one and repeat Point 1 to make the two rear forks. Allow to dry.

3. Using the template as a guide, snap the pastillage into the required lengths. Then, using thick sugar glue made from pastillage, glue the bike frame together.

4. Once the glue has dried, gradually add the remaining pieces until the frame is complete. You will probably find it necessary to support the pieces with foam whilst they dry.

5. Model a saddle from brown paste then paint the frame in colours of your choice.

Assembling the Bike
Place small balls of pastillage on either side of the centre of each wheel to help fill any gaps between the wheel and the forks. Glue in position, supporting the wheels/bike with foam. When dry place the bike on the cake and secure in position.

The Cyclist
To make the cyclist, use the medium-sized male template (see page 94) and the medium-sized adult head mould.

1. Model the head, facial features and torso of the cyclist as

described in Figure Modelling on pages 92-93.

2. Insert a dowel or pastillage sugar stick into the cake where the cyclist's body will be, then secure the torso on top. Model the legs (as described in Figure Modelling on pages 93) but excluding the feet and place in position, supporting them with pieces of foam, if necessary, whilst they dry.

Clothes
Trousers: Wrap some thinly rolled dark blue flowerpaste around each leg, bringing it up around the lower half of the torso. Cut off the excess paste at the waist and from the legs. The paste should fit the legs snugly.

Shoes: Model the cyclist's shoes from black modelling paste. They should be at least as long as his head. Use a ball tool to make holes in each shoe large enough to take the end of a leg; then, very gently lift each leg and place it in the appropriate shoe. Position the shoes and add trim and laces to each.

Shirt: Cover the upper body in coloured sections. Start with the light blue under the armpits. Glue thinly rolled pieces in position, then cut to the required shape with a small cutting wheel. Roll out some yellow flowerpaste and cut sections to fit the cyclist's front and back. Secure on the torso, smoothing the joins. For the zip, cut a thin black strip, attach it in position and mark the zip's teeth with a knife. Place two thin yellow strips on either side of the zip and around the top of the shirt for a collar.

48

Assembling the Cyclist

1. Model the arms and secure in position. Model a water bottle from a small amount of grey modelling paste and place in the cyclist's left hand. Allow the arms to harden. Wrap some thinly rolled dark blue flowerpaste around the top of each arm and over the shoulder, trim to shape with a cutting wheel and smooth the cut edge.

2. Paint on the facial features and model the hair. Allow the hair to harden, then take a 2.5cm (1") ball of orange modelling paste and shape it to form a cycling helmet. Secure in position and make ventilation holes by pressing a Dresden tool through the helmet. Use a food pen to add detail to the helmet and the cyclist's shirt. Finally, stick the head in position, adjusting the cut of the neck if necessary.

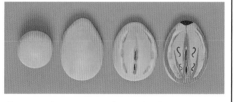

Completing the Cake

Make some mud (as below). Use a paintbrush to dab the mud over the bike and cyclist, then spread some over the bike trail, repeatedly passing a Dresden tool through it to create the impression of bike tracks. Finally, attach a ribbon around the board.

SPECIAL *Effects & Accessories*

Wheels

To achieve realistic spokes, I have used wires, so please ensure the cake's recipient is aware of this.

1. Take 18 white 28-gauge wires. Cut them to a length of 6cm (2 3/8") and wrap another wire around their centres to secure them all together. Repeat for the second wheel. Pull down half of the wires to form a radial pattern as shown. Glue a small ball of pastillage in the centre of each wheel and a strip of pastillage over the securing wires.

2. Once the pastillage has dried, use a pair of pliers to arrange the spokes by crossing them over in pairs: each spoke should cross two others.

3. Pull down the second set of wires and glue a pastillage ball in position as before. Arrange the spokes in the same pattern as for the first set, adjusting them so that their ends alternate with those below. Use pliers to move the tips of the two sets of spokes together so that they form a line; the straighter you can get this line, the more realistic the wheel will look.

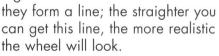

4. Place some softened white pastillage in a sugar shaper fitted with the medium-sized round disc. Extrude a length and place it over the tips of the spokes to form the wheel rim. Allow to dry thoroughly. Square off the rim by sticking on some more white pastillage: this will also help to hide any irregularities in the shape of the wheel.

5. Place some black modelling paste in a sugar shaper together with the half round disc. Extrude a length, secure it on top of the wheel rim and smooth it gently over the sides. When this has dried, pipe on the wheel tread with black royal icing using a No. 0 tube; tread patterns vary, so a series of dots is quite adequate.

6. Cover the spokes and wheel rim with Gildesol, then dust with edible silver lustre dust.

Mud

Let down some sugarpaste trimmings with boiled water, colour if necessary and apply as required.

Rocks

Rocks have many origins and are found in a wide range of colours; which colour you choose will therefore depend upon where the rocks are meant to be located. Whatever the predominant colour (e.g. red-orange sandstone, yellow-white chalk), you will find that the most realistic results are achieved by marbling the paste to include either subtle or bold changes in colour. Roll out marbled paste and cover the rocks. To make cracks and fissures, take the sharper end of a Dresden tool and press and drag it through the paste. Finer details can be added with a craft knife. Once the paste has hardened, dust the rocks to enhance their colour.

Materials

30cm x 22.5cm (12" x 9")
oblong cake drum
2 x 15cm (6") square Madeira
cakes
Buttercream
1.68kg (3lb 12oz) sugarpaste
670g (1lb 8oz) Mexican
Modelling Paste (MMP)
Paste colours:
Brown (SK Chestnut)
Green (SK Holly/Ivy)
Black
Red (SK Rose)
Orange (SK Marigold)
Yellow (SK Sunflower)
Black
Clear spirit, e.g. gin or vodka
Sugar glue
Gum tragacanth, Sugar sticks
Confectioners' glaze

Equipment

Pair of smoothers
Dresden tool
Straight edge
Corrugated cardboard
(for texturing the tiles)
Craft knife
2cm (³/₄") circle cutter
Sugar shaper
Ball tool
Small scissors
Paintbrushes, Ribbon
Food Pen: black

TEMPLATES USED

Horse Riding

Horses were first domesticated around 6000 years ago in southern Russia. It is believed that the Sumerians, settled in Babylonia, were the first to train their horses, using them to draw wheeled war chariots. In many parts of the world, horses became the most important means of transport but, by the late 19th and early 20th centuries, they were superseded first by trains and then by cars. The bond between these gentle animals and ourselves is still very strong and many people enjoy riding, be it for sport or pleasure.

Carving the Cake

Level the cakes, then sandwich

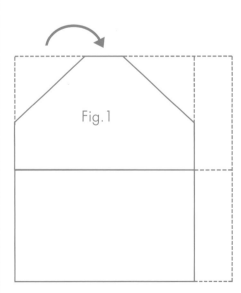

Fig. 1

one on top of the other with a layer of buttercream. Trim 2.5cm (1") from one side of the whole and shape the roof as illustrated (Fig.1), placing one of the cut sections on top to form the ridge. Position the cake on the board, towards the back and at an angle.

Covering the Cake

1. Colour 225g (8oz) sugarpaste pale grey-green. Spread a thin layer of buttercream over the front of the stable and cover just this area with the grey-green paste (this paste will form the door recess). Smooth and trim the icing flush with the sides and roof of the stable.

51

2. Colour 1.12kg (2lb 8oz) sugarpaste pale red-brown. Spread a thin layer of buttercream over the whole of the uncovered cake and brush cooled boiled water over the grey-green paste, except for where the stable door will be. This area should remain dry so that the door can easily be removed from the red-brown sugarpaste. Use the template as a guide (see page 97).

3. Roll out the red-brown sugarpaste and completely cover the cake, easing the paste over the corners. Trim the excess paste from the base of the cake and smooth the roof and sides.

Try to make the corners of the walls as sharp as possible by using two smoothers at right angles to one another.

4. With a straight edge (I used a set square), mark the brick courses by pressing this edge gently into the paste around the whole of the cake at approximately 7mm ($^1/_4$") intervals (S.E.p.54). Then mark the bricks using the sharper end of a Dresden tool.

5. Use the template and a craft knife to cut the stable door from the red-brown paste, revealing the grey-green paste below.

Allow to dry.

Timber Details

1. Add some brown paste colour to 225g (8oz) of the sugarpaste trimmings.

2. Make two thick sausages from this paste, each 15cm (6") long and 1cm ($^3/_8$") thick. Place these on the work surface and flatten one long edge of each with a smoother so that the sausages become more triangular in shape. Paint a line of sugar glue along the top of each side of the stable and place the flattened sausages in position, ensuring that their tops are in line with the roof. Use a smoother to check (see Fig.2).

Fig.2

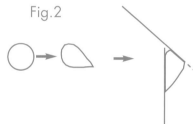

3. Add some gum tragacanth to the remaining brown paste to make modelling paste (approximately 1 teaspoon gum to 225g (8oz) sugarpaste) and allow the gum to take effect.

4. Thinly roll out some of this brown modelling paste and cut it into strips. Glue these around the door to make the frame and the beam above. Then, with a craft knife, mark the wood grain pattern. Using the template as a guide, make the two

JASPER

halves of the door, texture as before and glue in position. Model hinges from paste coloured black and attach.

Roof Tiles

Colour 280g (10oz) modelling paste pink-brown (I used a combination of SK Rose and Chestnut). Roll this out, then take a piece of corrugated cardboard (first varnished with confectioners' glaze and allowed to dry) and gently press it into the paste in order to texture it. Cut the paste into 1.5cm (⁵⁄₈") strips and glue them onto the roof in overlapping layers. Make the ridge tiles from a 15cm (6") long rolled piece of paste. Once secure, mark the joins in the tiles with a craft knife.

Painting the Stable

Dilute suitable paste colours in clear spirit and paint the walls, roof and timber (I used a range of colours, including SK Black, Rose, Chestnut, Marigold for the walls; Rose and Chestnut for the roof; and Chestnut for the timber)

The Cobbles

Colour 225g (8oz) modelling paste in various shades of grey and light brown and make the cobbles (S.E.p.54). Cover the board with 336g (12oz) light grey sugarpaste and continue as described in (S.E.p.54).

The Horse

1. Colour 28g (1oz) modelling paste pale brown and shape it into a horse's head, using the template and photographs as a guide.

2. Insert the small end of a ball tool into the nose to form the nostrils, then insert a sugar stick into the neck to lend support to the head once positioned on the cake. Allow to dry.

3. Take a small amount of dark

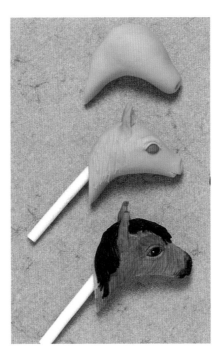

brown paste and make two eyeballs; secure these in position. Build up above the eye with pale brown paste as shown and make eyelids. Model ears and glue in position. Mark the mouth with a craft knife and trim away some paste from the lower jaw.

4. Gently insert the horse's head into the opening in the stable door and secure in position. You may find it easier first to prepare a hole for the sugar stick with a dowel.

5. Let down some pale brown sugarpaste with a little water until it is still thick enough to hold its shape but can be applied with a paintbrush. Paint this paste over the horse's head in the direction of his coat. Emphasise this effect by passing the sharper end of a Dresden tool through the let-down paste.

6. Colour some of the sugarpaste trimmings black and make the mane by pushing the black paste through the mesh disc of a sugar shaper. Colour the horse with diluted paste and/or dust colours.

Assembling the Cake

Model a riding hat, bales of straw, a bucket (S.E.p.54), then make the crop, tethering ring, brush and horseshoe, from leftover pieces of modelling paste. To make the bristles on the brush, cut into the paste with a sharp pair of small scissors. Make a small plaque to hang above the door and using a black food pen, inscribe it with the horse's name. Secure all the pieces in position and, finally, attach a ribbon around the board.

SPECIAL *Effects* & *Accessories*

Riding Hat

Make a 2.5cm (1") ball from black modelling paste and cut $1/3$ away, leaving a flat side which will form the underside of the hat. Extrude thin lengths of black paste from a sugar shaper, as for the mane, and cross two lengths over the top hat, finishing with a small ball. To make the brim, use a 2cm ($3/4$") circle cutter, cut as illustrated and place under the front of the hat.

Bucket

Using some of the roof tile trimmings, cut a 2cm ($3/4$") circle and a 1.5cm ($5/8$") deep strip to fit around the outer edge of the circle. Glue the strip in position, ensuring that it remains vertical, and allow to harden. Make a handle and rim from very thin strips of paste and secure in place. Paint the bucket if desired.

Bricks

Brickwork embossers are available and are very easy to use, though I often prefer the flexibility of marking my own bricks. To do this, press a straight edge into soft sugarpaste at regular

(approximately 7mm ($1/4$") intervals horizontally up the wall, to mark the brick

courses. Then press a Dresden tool vertically between the courses to mark the brickwork pattern. Once dry, the bricks can be painted or dusted to the colour required: I use a range of colours for this in order to enhance the effect of the brickwork.

Timber

Roll out brown modelling paste to the required thickness and cut to size. Take a craft knife and cut a wood-grain pattern into the paste. Once dry,

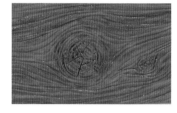

brush over the timber with diluted brown paste colour: the colour will sink into the cuts and the wood grain pattern will become more prominent.

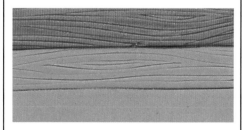

Cobblestones by Hand

Mix various colours of modelling paste together to make a marbled paste (S.E.p.69). Take very small amounts of the marbled paste and roll small pebbles. Once you have enough, allow them to dry thoroughly. Cover the area where the cobblestones are to go with a similarly coloured sugarpaste.

Brush the paste with sugar glue, then carefully place the cobbles in position. Gently press the cobbles into the paste with a smoother: this will cause the sugarpaste to spread slightly and some trimming may be required.

Bales of Straw: Oblong

Roll straw coloured paste into a thick sausage then, with a pair of smoothers, squash it together so that two sides become flat. Turn the shape over onto one of the flat sides and squash again to make a four-sided oblong shape. Mark lines to represent baler twine and, with a craft knife, mark the lengths of straw going across the bale. Using a Dresden tool, repeatedly indent the sides of the bale to represent the cut straw. Once dry, paint with diluted yellow-brown colour.

MORE SPECIAL
Effects

Roofing Tiles
Thinly roll out some pale brown modelling paste and cut circles using a small circle cutter. Arrange these in overlapping rows as shown. Once dry, apply a terracotta colour wash.

Slates
Thinly roll out some blue/grey modelling paste and cut into rectangles. Arrange these in overlapping rows as shown. Once dry, apply a blue/grey colour wash.

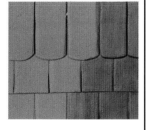

Thatch
Cover the building to be thatched with brown sugarpaste then, using a craft knife, cut repeatedly into the soft paste with long vertical strokes. Indent the lower edge of the thatch with the sharper end of a Dresden tool. Many thatched buildings have decorated patterns on top of their thatch; if you wish to add these, roll very thin sausages of the brown paste and arrange in your chosen pattern. Finally, apply a colour wash over the thatch to hghlight its texture.

Bales of Straw: Round
Model a wide cylinder from light brown modelling paste then, using a Dresden tool, mark a spiral pattern on the round ends of the bale. Cut into the paste with a craft knife to give the impression of the straw. Finally, apply a light brown colour wash.

Stooks
To make the sheaves of corn that make up the stook, roll thick sausages from pale brown modelling paste. Indent lines down each sausages using the sharper end of a Dresden tool and a craft knife. Take a small sharp pair of scissors and cut into one end to make ears of corn. Arrange three sheaves together as shown. Arrange thin lengths of paste around the centre of each sheaf to look as though they have been tied together. Finally, apply a colour wash.

Cobblestones
Using an Impression Mat:
This is a very quick and easy way to create cobblestones. Cover your board with sugarpaste, then press an impression mat gently but firmly into the paste. Repeat until the board is covered with cobblestones. Once the paste has hardened, colour it with diluted paste and/or dust colours.

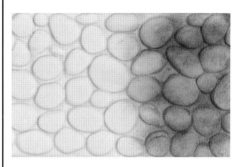

Brickwork Arch
Mark the bricks, then once the paste is firm, remove it from the door/window opening and from the arched area above the opening. Replace with a strip of soft paste into this arched area and indent the brickwork with a Dresden tool.

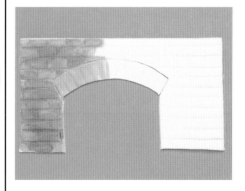

Quoining

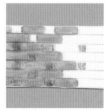

Flemish Bond

55

Materials

2 x 18cm (7") square cakes
40.5cm x 35.5cm (16 x 14") oval
board, 60g (2oz) pale brown pastillage
1.8kg (4lb) sugarpaste, coloured as
follows:1.12kg (2lb 8oz) white
280g (10oz) dark brown
168g (6oz) warm grey
225g (8oz) marbled green (see
Marbling on page 69)
865g (1lb 14½oz) Mexican Modelling
Paste (MMP), coloured as follows: 84g
(3oz) black
280g (10oz) pale brown (for the
timber), 168g (6oz) pale green (for the
roof and cabbages)
60g (2oz) terracotta
15g (1/2oz) olive green (for the seed
trays), 60g (2oz) flesh
28g (1oz) white
168g (6oz) mid green - for the compost
bin, 210g (7½oz) flowerpaste,
coloured as follows:
15g (½oz) dark blue
28g (1oz) mid blue
168g (6oz) pale green
Paste colours to colour the above
A range of green and brown dust
colours, Dust colours:
terracotta (SK Etruscan Brick), yellow
brown (SK Desert Storm)
Brown (SK Chestnut)
A range of greens (e.g. SK Fern, Forest
Green, Green Envy, Mint, Vine)
Squires Kitchen Edible Lustre Dust: Silver
, White fat, e.g. Trex or White Flora,
Cornflour, Spaghetti/sugar sticks
Gildesol, Sugar glue

Equipment

Craft knife, Sugar shaper
Pair of smoothers
Small circle cutters (Tinkertech)
Dresden tool, Ball tool
Piping tubes: Large star (to texture the
grass) and No. 2 or No. 3 (for cutting
daisies), plus a selection to be used as
formers for the pots, Pestle and
mortar/electric grinder
Paintbrushes, Mini stitching wheel
Double-sided veiners (to vein the
cabbages and cauliflower)
Cutters: 3 orchid or similar (for the
cauliflower); daisy leaf or similar (for the
tomato); small leaf
(for the plants in pots)

TEMPLATE USED

Gardening

The earliest recorded gardens are those of the ancient Egyptians, but it was not until the time of the Romans that gardens became an important part of domestic life. The Romans became very knowledgeable horticulturists, growing a large range of vegetables and plants. Following the collapse of the Roman Empire, however, this knowledge virtually died out and it was not until the end of the Dark Ages that plants began to be cultivated again in monasteries and in fortified buildings. Up until the early 16th century, gardens had essentially been utilitarian; from that time onwards, however, decorative gardens became popular, influenced by the Italian and French renaissance and the English landscape movement. Today, gardening is a hobby enjoyed by many: it is no longer the prerogative of the privileged, as most of us have a garden, no matter how small, in which we can grow plants.

Shed Door

Roll out some of the pale brown pastillage to a thickness of 2mm (¹/₁₆") and cut out a 6cm x 12.6cm (2 ³/₈" x 5") rectangle. Using a straight edge, divide the door into six panels, then mark the woodgrain with a craft knife (S.E.p.54). Repeat this on the reverse side of the door. Cut 5mm (¹/₄") wide strips of pastillage and attach these horizontally and diagonally to the door. Note that the middle strip is slightly wider than the others. Mark the woodgrain and place on foam to dry.

Carving the Cake

Level the cakes, then sandwich one on top of the other with a layer of buttercream. Trim 5cm (2") off one side to give the shed a width of 12.5cm (5"), then shape the roof, placing an additional

section on top as in Fig.1. Position the cake on the board as in Fig.2.

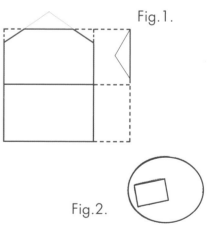

Fig.1.

Fig.2.

Covering the Cake and Board

1. Spread a thin layer of buttercream over the sides of the shed. Roll out the white sugarpaste, cut four pieces approximately the shape of each

side and place the pieces in position, cutting each flush with the adjoining sides. Cover the roof in the same manner.

2. Thinly roll out some black modelling paste and cut a 7.3cm x 13.8cm ($2^7/_8$" x $5^1/_2$") rectangle to make the door opening. Stick this centrally to the front of the shed. Next, cut out an 8cm x 4.5cm ($3^1/_8$" x $1^3/_4$") rectangle for the window and secure it centrally in position on the side of the shed.

3. Roll out the dark brown sugarpaste and cover the garden area to the side of the shed.

4. Make the paved area with the 168g (6oz) grey sugarpaste (S.E.p.59).

5. Thinly roll out some pale brown modelling paste and cut 1.5cm ($^1/_2$") wide strips. Mark the woodgrain on each strip with a craft knife (S.E.p.54), then attach these in overlapping horizontal layers on the sides of the cake, cutting the ends of each strip flush with the white sugarpaste on the adjoining sides. This will leave space for the corner timbers. Also cut the strips so that they abut the black modelling paste of the window and door openings.

6. Soften some of the pale brown modelling paste and place it in a sugar shaper fitted with a square disc. Extrude lengths of paste and secure these around the door and window openings. Make the vertical timber pieces to be positioned at the corners of the shed in the same fashion, using a pair of smoothers to ensure that the timbers are straight and vertical. To make a lip on the roof

under which to tuck the felt, attach an extruded length to the top of the longer shed sides and shape with a smoother so that the upper edge is in line with the roof.

7. Thinly roll out the pale green modelling paste. Measure the roof and cut out a shape that will completely cover it, also allowing for tucking under the sides. Place on the cake and smooth. Then cut out a rectangle the same length as one side of the roof and place it over the top of the shed so that it hangs partially down both sides of the roof. Once dry, texture the roof with sugarpaste dust (S.E.p.59).

8. Cut out four more strips of pale brown modelling paste and glue these so that they cover the area where the roofing felt joins the front and back of the shed. Use a smoother to press the strips flat, then trim to ensure that they are straight. Finally, cut the woodgrain pattern into the paste.

9. Dilute some brown paste colour (SK Chestnut) in cooled boiled water and colour wash the timber to bring out the grain and darken the shed. Do not forget to colour wash the door as well!

10. Make the cut grass (S.E.p.70).

11. Apply the soil to the dark brown sugarpaste (S.E.p.59).

The Gardener

Legs: Using the flesh-coloured modelling paste and the small male template, model the gardener's legs (see Figure Modelling on pages 93-94),

extending each leg up to waist height. Bend each leg at the knee and hip as shown. Insert a length of dry spaghetti or a narrow sugar stick into each leg to help give support, then leave the legs on their sides to dry.

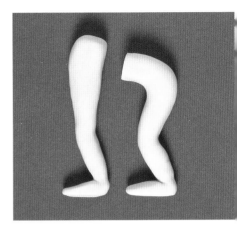

58

Shoes: Once the legs are dry, thinly roll out some dark blue flowerpaste (SK Bluebell) and cover the front of each foot, trimming the paste to shape with small scissors. Next cut two small strips and wrap around each heel to complete the shoes.

Trousers: Colour some flowerpaste a mid blue. Thinly roll it out and cut two 5cm (2") wide strips. Wrap these loosely around each leg so that the join is on the inner leg; do not worry about the top of the legs as these are covered by the jacket. Run a mini stitch wheel along all the seams.

Assembling the Gardener

Attach the legs in position on the cake, adding some more paste to round off the back. Once the legs are secure, attach a length of thinly rolled dark green flowerpaste over the back and sides for the jacket.

Assembling the Cake

Make all the accessories (S.E.pp.59-61). Using thick sugar glue, attach the door to the doorframe. Insert the bamboo canes into the door opening, securing them with glue, and arrange the pots, tumbling polystyrene plant cells, seed trays and spade. Place the bamboo canes in position at the side of the shed by pushing them gently but firmly into the soil. Then assemble the tomato plants (S.E.p.61). Then position the vegetables and the rabbit. Once you are happy with their positions, secure them all in place. Finally, make a hose pipe from softened pale yellow paste extruded from a sugar shaper fitted with the small round disc.

SPECIAL *Effects* & *Accessories*

Roofing Felt

Colour some modelling paste to match the shade of the felt required. Thinly roll it out and cover the roof in overlapping layers. Take the leftover paste and grate it with a kitchen grater before placing it in a warm, dry place to harden completely. Grind the paste once hard, using either a pestle and mortar or an electric grinder to produce a fine, coloured dust. Brush

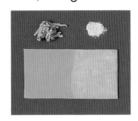

sugar glue over the felt, then sprinkle on the ground paste. Allow the glue to set before brushing off the excess dust.

Stone Paving

Colour some sugarpaste a warm grey using black and yellow paste colours. Roll this out and cut oblongs and squares of various sizes. Position these pieces on the board, leaving a slight gap between each piece and the next (see step). Let down some of the leftover grey sugarpaste, adding enough water so that the paste can be applied with a paintbrush. Darken it by adding more colour then, with a loaded paintbrush, encourage the let-down paste

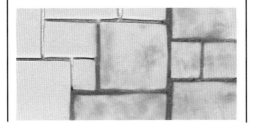

between the paving slabs. Next, take a damp cloth and wipe over the surface of the slabs to help spread the paste into the grooves and to give more colour and texture to the paving.

Soil

Take a kitchen grater and grate some dark brown sugarpaste together with some of a lighter colour and leave to dry. Once hard, briefly grind the grated paste in a pestle and mortar so that the paste remains in small lumps rather than becoming a dust. Cover the ground with sugar glue and sprinkle on the soil. Allow the glue to set, then brush off the excess.

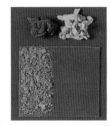

Cauliflower

Roll eight 1.75cm (³/₄") balls of white modelling paste. Take a pan scourer and indent the top of each ball to represent the cauliflower's florets, then leave to dry. Make three small leaves from thinly rolled pale green flowerpaste using a suitable cutter (e.g. the top of an orchid cutter). Vein with a suitable veiner, then thin the edges of each leaf with a ball tool to give the leaves some movement.

Attach the leaves around the cauliflower as shown. Make two medium-sized and five large leaves, attach as appropriate, then leave to dry. Repeat as necessary. Dust the leaves with a range of greens (e.g. SK Fern, Mint and Green Envy).

Cabbages

Roll six 1.5cm (⁵⁄₈″) balls of green modelling paste and leave to harden. Thinly roll out some pale green flowerpaste and cut three 2cm (³⁄₄″) circles. Vein each with a suitable double-sided veiner (cabbage leaf veiners are available, but use whatever you have in your toolbox, e.g. lamium veiner).

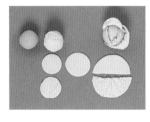

Attach one leaf, with the veining uppermost over the top of the ball, then arrange the other two around the first, curling the top of each leaf over (see step). Cut two 2.5cm (1″) circles, vein, attach and shape as before. Then cut two or three 3.5cm (1³⁄₈″) circles, halve and vein, then attach to the cabbage, shaping each leaf once in position. Repeat for the other cabbages and leave to dry. Dust the cabbages in a range of greens (e.g. SK Vine, Green Envy and Forest Green), starting with the lightest in the centre.

Compost Bin

Take 168g (6oz) green modelling paste and roll it into a large cone with a base diameter of 5cm (2″). Cut the top so that the bin has a height of 5.5cm. Mark the ridges in the side of the bin with a Dresden tool, then enlarge them with a ball tool. Mark the horizontal lines around the bin with the sharper end of the Dresden tool, then transfer the bin to the board. For the lid, roll the

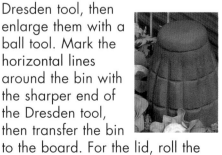

remaining paste into a ball, place it on a flat surface and smooth it into a flat dome shape. Then cut it into a circle with the 3.5cm (1³⁄₄″) cutter, gently smooth the cut edge and stick in position on top of the bin.

Pots & Plants

1. Thinly roll out the terracotta-coloured modelling paste and cut into strips about 2cm (³⁄₄″) wide. Brush the outside surfaces of the piping tubes with white fat, then dust with cornflour to prevent the paste from sticking. Take a strip of paste and wrap it around a tube, cutting the paste to give a neat vertical join, and leave to dry. Repeat to make other pots of varying heights. When the paste has hardened slightly, remove the pots from the tube and

leave to dry completely. Cut small circles from rolled out terracotta-coloured paste for the base of each pot and make drainage holes in their centres. Then glue a base to the body of each pot. Finish the pots by dusting with terracotta-coloured dust (SK Etruscan Brick).

2. To make the pot plants, first model solid pots by pressing a rounded cone of terracotta-coloured paste into a large piping tube. Remove the paste and cut the top flat, then stand

the pot upright to dry and repeat. To make the plants themselves, cut out leaves from thinly rolled green flowerpaste using a small leaf

cutter (or part of a larger one) and arrange them in the top of the pots. Once dry, dust the plants with green and the pots with terracotta dust.

Bamboo Canes

Soften some of the pastillage and place it into a sugar shaper fitted with a small round disc. Extrude lengths, straighten and leave to dry. To create the impression of bamboo canes, dust the lengths with a yellow/brown dust (SK Desert Storm), then with a brown (SK Chestnut) at intervals along each length.

Seed Trays

Thinly roll out some dark green modelling paste, then cut out and make the seed trays as illustrated.

Polystyrene Plant Cells

Roll out some white modelling paste, then make holes in the paste to represent the rows of plant cells. Do not worry about the precise number of cells, as these vary. Once you have a sufficient number of holes, cut out the 2.5cm x 1.5cm (1″ x ¹⁄₂″) trays.

Daisies

These are very easy to make! Thinly roll out some white flowerpaste, then take a No. 2 or No. 3 piping tube and press the narrow end into the paste to make tiny circles. Attach these to the 'grass', then take a yellow food pen and place a dot of yellow in the centre of each flower.

Spade

Soften some pastillage and place it in a sugar shaper fitted with a medium-sized round disc. Extrude a short length for the shaft of the spade. Whilst this is drying, thinly roll out some more pastillage and, using the template (see page 95), cut out the blade. Carefully place the top section over the partially dried shaft and gently shape the blade over it. Prop up the blade with small pieces of foam to achieve its characteristic shape and leave to dry. Once dry, apply Gildesol and silver lustre dust to the blade.

Tomato Plants (stylised)

Cut leaves from thinly rolled green flowerpaste (using a daisy leaf cutter, for example) and arrange them in groups of four as shown. Cover the leaves with plastic until needed. To assemble make small green balls of flowerpaste and glue one at the foot of each bamboo cane. Then place a group of four leaves

on top of each ball and arrange them as necessary. Repeat until the plants are of the height required, then top each with two leaves joined together as shown. Dust once dry.

Rabbit

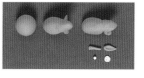

Roll a 1.5cm (⁵⁄₈") ball of light brown modelling paste and extend one end to form a pear-shape. Use a sharp pair of scissors to cut into the paste to form the two front legs. Use a Dresden tool to define the shoulders and neck, then hand-model the face. Make the ears from small elongated balls of paste and attach them to the top of the head. Next, make the tail from a small ball of white modelling paste and texture it with the pointed end of the Dresden tool. When the rabbit is dry, paint his eyes with paste colours and dust the inside of his ears and nose with pink dust colour.

MORE SPECIAL
Effects

Crazy Paving

A variation of stone paving. Colour some sugarpaste in a range of colours. Make randomly shaped flat stones, attach them to the board and continue as for stone paving.

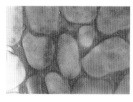

Brickwork Paving

Cover the board with sugarpaste, then use an oblong cutter to mark a herringbone pattern in the soft paste. Fill in as for stone paving.

Corrugated Roofing

Roll out some modelling paste and cut a rectangle slightly larger than the area of the roof to be covered. Keeping the paste on the board, use barbecue skewers to shape it as shown, then allow the paste to harden. Once the paste retains it shape, cut it to size and transfer it to the roof.

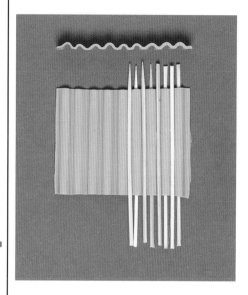

Quick Soil

Cover the ground with brown sugarpaste and, whilst it is still soft, texture it with a sponge, as shown, or even a stiff bristled brush. Apply a colour wash to highlight the texture.

Materials

28cm (11") cake drum
6 egg Madeira cake, cooked in
two 15cm (6") round tins
1.34kg (3lb) sugarpaste,
coloured as follows:
670g(1½lb) marbled green
(SK Sunflower, Holly/Ivy
and Black)
670g (1½lb) orange
(SK Marigold, Sunflower
and Daffodil)
224g (8oz) MexicanModelling
Paste (MMP), coloured as
follows:
14g (½oz) dark brown
(SK Bulrush)
28g (1oz) brown (SK Chestnut)
56g (2oz) blue (SK Bluebell)
56g (2oz) red (SK Poinsettia)
56g (2oz) cream (tiny amount
SK Chestnut)
14g (½oz) grey
4 x 2cm (¾") sugar sticks
Pastillage, small amount
Squires Kitchen Edible Lustre
Dust: Silver
Gildesol, Sugar glue
Clear spirit, e.g. gin or vodka

Equipment

Knife for carving
Waxed paper
Dresden tool
Material (for texturing basket)
Sugar shaper
Paintbrush
Ribbon (to go around
the board)

TEMPLATES USED

Ballooning

The first manned balloon flight took place in France in 1783. Today, ballooning is a popular sport, with balloon races and rallies being held throughout the world. The balloons themselves are made from lightweight synthetic fabrics, come in many shapes and sizes and often display logos of the companies that sponsor them.

The beauty of a partially inflated hot air balloon is that it is never static: it moves and twists as though it has a mind of its own. Your cake, therefore, does not necessarily have to be symmetrical and can boast bulges and impressions wherever you choose to have them. Likewise, when covering your cake, there is no need to achieve a perfectly even finish to the sugarpaste: you could even mark creases in the fabric of the balloon.

Covering the Board

Cover the board with green marbled sugarpaste: texture and paint (S.E.p.70).

Carving the Cake

TIP: Carve this cake from frozen. First of all, level the cakes. Then

place Template 1 (see page 95) on top of each cake and cut around it. Stack the cakes, sticking them together with buttercream. Wrap Template 2 (see page 95) around half of the cake. Cut away the excess cake from the front of the balloon and mark the balloon's centre with a cocktail stick (Fig.1). Using Template 2 as a guide, divide the balloon into six sections

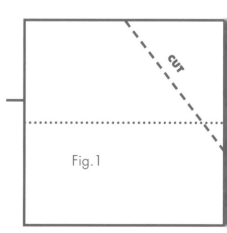

Fig.1

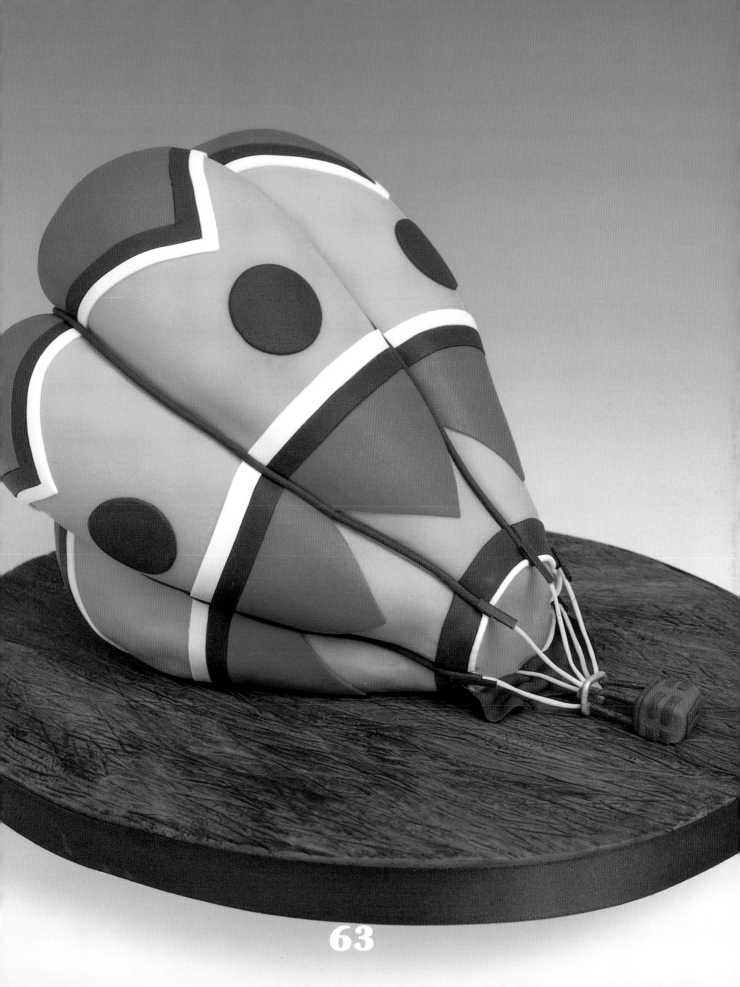

from this centre, marking each with a knife cut. Shape each section, carving slowly and carefully, using the photographs as a guide and cutting into the marked lines.

Covering the Cake

Place the cake upside-down on waxed paper. Cover the two lower panels of the balloon individually with orange sugarpaste, using a thin layer of buttercream to stick the paste to the cake. Trim away the excess paste and smooth the join between the panels. Turn the cake the right way up and cover the remaining panels. Cut a 4cm (1¼") circle from orange sugarpaste and stick it onto the entrance of the balloon. Trim the outer edge so that it is flush with sides of the balloon, smoothing as necessary.

Decorating the Balloon

1. Hot air balloons come in a wonderful array of colours and designs, so you can choose to create your own design (for ideas, see S.E.p.65) or to decorate the balloon as I have, using Template 3 (see page 95) as a guide.

2. Cut the required shapes from thinly rolled modelling paste. Stick into position with sugar glue, trimming the sides to form a neat join with the next panel.

3. Extrude six 25cm (9½") lengths of blue modelling paste from a sugar shaper fitted with the smallest round disc. Attach these lengths between each of the balloon panels to conceal the joins. Cut small tabs from thinly rolled blue modelling paste and stick around the entrance to the balloon.

The Basket

1. Take a small amount of modelling paste and shape it into a 1.5cm x 1.5cm x 1cm (⅝" x ⅝" x ⅜") oblong. Texture the sides by pressing some material into the paste to represent basket weave. Cut small strips of thinly rolled dark brown modelling paste to make the leather straps and stick these to the sides of the basket as shown. Cut some more and attach these to the base of the basket to form a rectangle.

2. Place glue on the end of each sugar stick and insert these into the four corners of the basket so that they slant slightly inwards. Allow to dry.

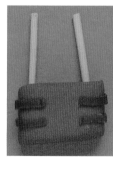

3. Take a small amount of dark brown modelling paste, roll it into a thin sausage and place it around the top of the basket. Make a similar sausage from pastillage. Balance the basket upside-down so that it rests on the sugar sticks, then stick the

pastillage around the top of the sugar sticks to make the frame to hold the burner. Once dry, apply Gildesol and then silver lustre dust to the burner frame

and paint the sugar sticks with dark brown paste diluted in clear spirit. Make the burner by rolling a sausage of grey modelling paste just thick enough to fit within the burner frame. Cut the end from the sausage (this is the burner)

and, with the end of a paintbrush, make a hole in the cut side. Stick in position.

Assembling the Cake

Place the cake on the board. To make the skirt cut a 6cm (2¼") circle from thinly rolled blue modelling paste, halve and stick one half to the lower panels of the balloon's entrance, gathering the paste up slightly. Place the basket in position approximately 5cm (2") away from the balloon. To make the cables that suspend the basket from the balloon, roll six very fine sausages from grey modelling paste and attach with sugar glue. Make the balloon's tether in a similar manner and attach to the top of the balloon. Finally, place the ribbon around the board.

SPECIAL Effects & Accessories

Inlay Panel Designs

65

Materials

30cm (12") round cake board
A cake cooked in a 1¼ litre (2 pint)
pudding basin
Buttercream
1.46kg (3lb 4oz) sugarpaste
194g (7oz) Mexican Modelling Paste
(MMP), coloured as follows:
112g (4oz) flesh
28g (1oz) black
28g (1oz) cream
28g (1oz) brown (SK Chestnut)
Paste colours:to colour the above
for painting the face
a range of greens
a range of blues
168g (6oz) pastillage
Dust colours to colour the reeds (e.g.
SK Shady Moss, Forest Green, Green
Envy, Leaf Green, Fern, Vine)
Flowerpaste: 28g (1oz) green
(SK Holly/Ivy),
28g (1oz) pale green,
42g (1½oz) dark blue (SK Bluebell)
Piping gel
Confectioners' glaze
Uncooked spaghetti
Sugar glue

Equipment

Waxed paper
Cutting wheel, Sugar shaper
Holly Products Adult Head Mould
Dresden tool
2cm (¾") circle cutter
Large circle cutter, e.g. 5cm (2")
Paintbrushes
Fine piping tube, e.g. No.1 or 0
Small flower/leaf cutters
Ribbon

Birdwatching

It is possible to watch birds in virtually any location including city centres and inhospitable regions of the world. Many people feed the birds in winter and enjoy watching them build their nests in spring. They marvel at the return of the swallows and young water birds taking their first swim. But for some, birdwatching (or twitching, as it is also known) is an all consuming hobby and it is for these people that I have designed this cake.

Covering the Board

Take 900g (2lb) sugarpaste and colour portions various shades of blue, also preparing small amounts of green and brown. Roughly knead these together to produce a marbled effect (see Marbling on page 69). Cover the board and leave to dry.

Covering the Cake

Level the cake and place on waxed paper. Colour 560g (1lb 4oz) sugarpaste in a variety of greens and combine them to make a marbled paste. Spread a thin layer of buttercream over the cake, then cover with the marbled paste, placing the paste in such a way that any lines in the marbling go vertically up, rather than horizontally across the cake. Once dry, attach the cake to the back of the board with a small amount of buttercream.

Reeds

To make the reeds, colour the pastillage in two shades of green (S.E.p.70).

Binoculars

Make a pair of binoculars
(S.E.p.69).

The Twitcher

1. Torso: Using the largest male template (see page 94) and 70g (2½oz) flesh-coloured modelling paste, model the upper half of the man's torso (i.e. from the neck to the waist). Attach this centrally to the top of the cake, then insert small pieces of dry spaghetti into each arm socket (to support the arms at a later stage) and a longer piece through the body to support the neck.

2. Head: Roll a 3.5cm (1³/₈") diameter ball from flesh-coloured modelling paste and, using the largest head mould, model the twitcher's head (see Figure Modelling on pages 92-93). Place on top of the body and allow to dry.

3. Face: Once the head has dried, add ears, then paint and dust the facial detail.

4. Hair: Thinly roll out some brown modelling paste, then use the circle cutter to cut repeatedly into the paste (see page 93.) Cut small pieces from this textured paste and gently squash the ends towards one another to produce waves in the paste. Attach these to the head in a suitable hairstyle.

5. T Shirt: Roll out a thin strip of cream modelling paste and use a circle cutter to remove a half circle from one edge of the strip. Glue the strip to the front of the man: the cut away paste should fit neatly around his neck to form the T-shirt.

6. Shirt: Thinly roll out some olive green flowerpaste, cut a strip to make the shirt collar wrap around his neck and glue in position. Then cut a 2cm (³/₄") wide strip, remove a 'V' from the top end of the strip and stick the 'V' under the collar to form the front of the shirt. Give the shirt movement by ensuring that it is not stuck to all areas of the body, then trim off the excess paste. Let down some of the black modelling paste and pipe the zip using a fine tube.

7. Jacket Body: Thinly roll out a rectangle of blue flowerpaste and wrap it around the mans' body, trim it to shape. Leave the front of the jacket open and encourage the paste to form folds, giving movement to the jacket. Make a small cylinder of paste, attach it to the top of the jacket for the collar and texture it with the sharper end of a Dresden tool.

8. Arms: Model the arms from flesh-coloured modelling paste Attach to the shoulders and place the hands around the binoculars. Support all the pieces in position with foam until the glue has dried.

9. Jacket Sleeves: Once the arms are firm, roll out two 10cm (4") long strips of blue flowerpaste and curve one end of each strip. Paint sugar glue around the top of the shoulders, the elbow and the wrist. Attach the curved end of one of the strips to a shoulder, ensuring that the join with the jacket body is neat. Attach the other end of the strip to the wrist, then ease the strip around the arm, allowing it form creases. Join the edges of the strip together under the arm, cutting off excess paste as necessary. Repeat for the second arm. Make the cuffs from thin strips of paste and texture by cutting repeatedly into the paste with a cutting wheel. Glue in place.

Assembling the Cake

1. Let down some of the green sugarpaste trimmings with a little water. Starting at the top of the cake around the twitcher, attach the reeds by pushing them firmly into the sugarpaste; then, with a paintbrush, apply some of the let-down sugarpaste around the base of each reed to ensure that it is held securely. Gradually bring the reeds down over the sides of the cake and into the water, using let-down blue paste to secure them.

2. Make and place a nest between the reeds (see below).

3. Make some water plants by thinly rolling out some green flowerpaste and using small flower cutters to cut leaf shapes (e.g. small blossom and Daphne cutters). Texture these with a Dresden tool, then arrange them randomly around the base of the reeds.

4. Apply piping gel to the board with a paintbrush, using the brush to create ripples.

5. Finally, attach a ribbon around the board.

SPECIAL *Effects* & *Accessories*

Marbling

Wonderful effects can be achieved by marbling sugarpaste. To create marbled paste, roughly mix a number of different coloured pastes together (not too much otherwise the effect will be lost), then roll the paste out and use as required. Results depend upon how many colours are used and in what proportion, as well as on how you mix and roll out the paste. Two methods are illustrated: the first makes a streaked pattern and the second a more random one. Experiment and see which patterns you prefer.

TIP: Once you have roughly mixed the colours together, cut through the paste and roll it out with the cut surface uppermost. You will find that a more intricate pattern develops this way.

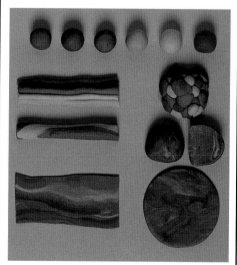

Birds Nest

Roll a 3cm (1¼") ball from cream-coloured modelling paste. Flatten and indent the centre to form the basic nest shape. Indent the sides with the sharper end of a Dresden tool and leave to dry. Paint the nest with a variety of diluted paste colours as shown. Model eggs and, once dry, place them in the nest.

Binoculars

Model these from black modelling paste as shown, glaze the lenses and, once the pieces are dry, glue all the sections together.

Reeds

To make reeds that are realistic, colour half of the pastillage light green and half dark green. Thinly roll out some of the pastillage and cut some reeds in various lengths and widths (a cutting wheel is the ideal tool for this as it cuts cleanly through the pastillage). Place the reeds on foam, giving them movement as you do so, and allow to dry thoroughly. Repeat until you have enough for your needs, then dust with various shades of green to give a realistic effect.

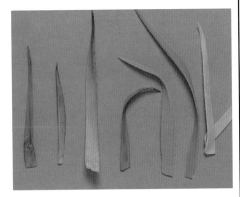

MORE SPECIAL
Effects

Grass

There are many ways of making grass depending on the effect you wish to achieve. Listed below are the methods I have used for the cakes in this book.

Textured Rough Grass

Roll out some marbled sugarpaste and cover the cake drum. Texture this with the sharper end of a Dresden tool, cutting into the paste in various directions. Additional texture can be added by pressing a new scouring pad onto the cut paste. Once the grass is dry, apply a green colour wash by diluting paste colour in clear spirit. This gives more definition and colour to the finished grass.

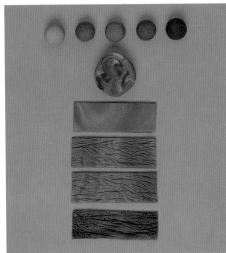

Tufts of Grass

Fill a sugar shaper with softened green sugarpaste fitted with a mesh disc. Squeeze out about 1cm (³/₈") of paste from the shaper and attach the resulting tuft of grass to the cake. Alternatively, roll a ball of sugarpaste, place it on  the inside of a kitchen sieve and gently press the ball through the mesh. Remove the grass with a small palette knife and place on the cake.

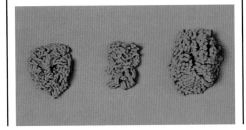

Cut Grass

Cover the lawn/playing field area with marbled green sugarpaste. Use a large star piping tube repeatedly to indent the surface of the paste. You will find that this makes the marbling look more like natural changes in the colour of the grass. When dry, brighten the colour of the grass by  applying a wash of diluted green paste colour.

Striped Lawn

To make a striped lawn, texture a strip as for cut grass, but this time hold the tube at a 60 degree angle. Then texture adjacent strips holding the tube in the opposite direction. Once dry, apply a colour wash in different shades as shown.

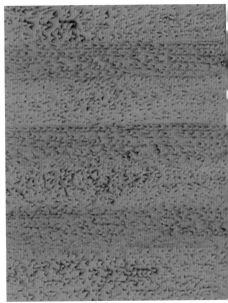

Quick Textured Grass

Cover the grass area with green sugarpaste. Take a clean, dry, stiff bristled kitchen brush and press it repeatedly into the paste until you are happy with the effect. How deep and at what angle you indent the paste will determine the final texture achieved. Try also experimenting with different brushes: a bottlebrush is very effective, for example. Once the grass is dry, paint over the cake with various diluted green pastes to brighten it.

Shrubs

These can be made from cake or from sugarpaste, depending on the size of shrub required. If using cake, carve it to create the basic shape; if making a smaller shrub, model sugarpaste to an appropriate shape. Next, cover the cake or modelled sugarpaste with green sugarpaste. This can then be textured in a number of ways: repeatedly pushing the sharper end of a Dresden tool into the paste and dragging it downwards is very effective, but

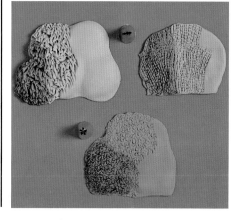

other effects can be achieved using a variety of piping tubes. See what you have in your toolbox and experiment by pressing the tubes into the paste at various angles. Once the shrub has been textured, leave to dry, then paint with diluted green paste colours to add depth to the texturing.

Materials

35.5cm x 41cm (14"x16")
rectangular board
2 x 20cm (8") square
Madeira cake
Buttercream
3.14kg (7lb) sugarpaste
Flowerpaste: white (small amount)
Colours to decorate the mug
Paste colours:
Black
Yellow (SK Sunflower)
Orange (SK Marigold)
Red and pink (SK Fuchsia
and Rose)
Purple (SK Claret)
Brown (SK Chestnut)
Mexican Modelling Paste (MMP):
84g (3oz) pale brown
56g (2oz) purple
225g (8oz) white
8g (1/4oz) black
Small amount of runout icing
Gildesol
Squires Kitchen Edible
Lustre Dust: Copper
Gum tragacanth
Clear spirit, e.g. gin or vodka
Sugar glue

Equipment

Food pen: black
Waxed paper, Smoother
Material (to texture board)
Small circle cutter
2.5cm (1") circle cutter
1cm (3/8") square cutter
Straight edge
Natural sponge
Paintbrushes
Set square (or similar)
4mm spacers
Letter cutters, Ribbon

TEMPLATES USED

COMPUTERS

You either love them or you hate them. I must admit to being rather attached to mine, whereas my husband is a true technophobe, preferring only to come into contact with them when he absolutely must.Computers have evolved from mechanical calculating machines, the first one of these being devised in 1642 by the French philosopher Pascal. But it was not until the Second World War, when the first electronic computer, Colossus, was built to crack enemy codes, that any great advances were made. After the war, computers really began to develop. In the 1970s microchip technology reduced the size of computers and, for the first time, personal computers came onto the market. Today computers play a very important role in our lives and rank as one of the most important machines ever invented.

Carving the Cake

Level the cakes and cut as shown. Use buttercream to secure the cut sections in place as follows:

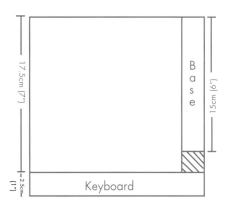

1. Make the base by stacking the two base sections together and cutting the top section diagonally down to the lower section as shown in Fig.1. Flip the cut-away portion over and position it behind the other section. Place the base on waxed paper.

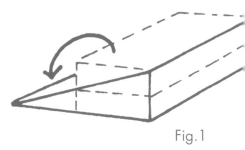

Fig.1

2. Stack the two main cakes on top of the base as shown and cut away the back section (Fig.2).

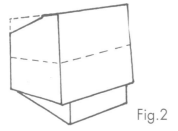

Fig.2

3. To make the keyboard, position the two keyboard sections of the cake end to end on waxed paper and cut to a length of 23cm (9"). Then cut diagonally down from the long top edge to the lower edge as shown in Fig.3.

Fig.3

Covering the Cake and Board

Use buttercream to stick the sugarpaste to the cake, spreading it thinly over the part you are about to cover.

1. Colour 1.5kg (3lb) sugarpaste light grey and cover the cake board. Place a suitable piece of material on top of the paste and rub over the surface with a smoother to give the board texture.

2. Use the board trimmings to make a strip 5cm (2") wide and 1cm (3/8") deep. Wrap this strip around and flush with what will become the screen.

3. Cover the front of the cake (the screen) with 450g (1lb) white sugarpaste.

4. Colour 1.5kg (3lb) sugarpaste grey, adding a touch of yellow to make a warm shade of grey. Use a small amount of this to cover the base, trimming it to shape.

5. Take approximately 450g (1lb) of the warm grey sugarpaste and roll it out into an 8cm (3") wide strip. Cut one of the long edges straight, then wrap the side of the strip around the sides of the screen, placing the cut edge flush with the screen itself. Neatly tuck the other side of the strip over the edge of the strip created in Point 2 and cut away any excess paste.

6. Cover the back of the cake with the warm grey, cutting all edges flush with the sides. Next, cover the remaining parts of the top and sides with a 13cm (5¼") wide strip, this time cutting the paste flush with the back of the cake.

7. For the front edging to the screen, place a line of glue around the outside of the screen, then place a rolled out piece of paste on top of the screen. Trim all the edges flush with the sides, then cut away the paste 2cm (3/4") in from the edge to reveal the screen underneath, cutting the corners away with a small circle cutter.

8. To finish off the cut edges on the sides and back of the cake, place some warm grey paste together with the medium-sized ribbon disc into the sugar shaper and extrude lengths to go on top of these cut edges. Secure in position.

The Computer Screen

1. Sponge and stipple the screen with a variety of colours, starting with the lightest in the centre and working outwards to the darkest.

2. Using white flowerpaste, cut out the letters for your chosen message and attach to the screen once they are firm enough to hold their shape.

3. Take 8g (1/4oz) of black modelling paste and place it in a sugar shaper with the medium-sized ribbon disc. Extrude some paste and stick it around the screen, making the inner corners square with a set square or similar. To finish off the screen, place some grey paste and the small round disc in the sugar shaper, extrude a length and glue around the screen.

74

Assembling the Cake

Make the mouse mat, the diary, the keyboard, the mouse and the mug (S.E.p.75). Position all the component parts of the cake on the board. Put some warm grey paste and the medium-sized round disc in the sugar shaper and extrude a length to go around the base of the cake. Also extrude lengths to make leads for the keyboard and mouse. Finally, place a length of ribbon around the board.

SPECIAL *Effects* *& Accessories*

Mouse Mat - Sponging

1. Thinly roll out 60g (2oz) of white modelling paste and cut it into a 10cm x 12.5cm (4"x 5") rectangle. Round the corners using a 2.5cm (1") circle cutter and allow to dry.

2. Mouse mats have all sorts of designs on them, so you can decorate yours as you wish. I chose to have a bright yet simple sponged design, using four colours that would complement my screen design. Start by sponging on the yellow and follow this with the orange as illustrated; then add the red and, finally, a deep pink. Leave to dry thoroughly.

Diary

Roll out 140g (5oz) of white modelling paste to a thickness

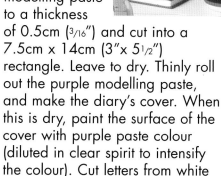

of 0.5cm (³/₁₆") and cut into a 7.5cm x 14cm (3"x 5½") rectangle. Leave to dry. Thinly roll out the purple modelling paste, and make the diary's cover. When this is dry, paint the surface of the cover with purple paste colour (diluted in clear spirit to intensify the colour). Cut letters from white flowerpaste. When dry, apply a layer of Gildesol and copper lustre dust. Position the letters on the cover.

Keyboard

Cover the keyboard with the remaining warm grey sugarpaste. Add gum tragacanth to the trimmings to make modelling paste (approximately 1 teaspoon/225g (8oz) sugarpaste. Roll out the modelling paste between 4mm spacers and, using a 1cm (³/₈") square cutter, cut out keys. To give them a concave surface gently press a small cylindrical object (e.g. a pencil) into the surface of

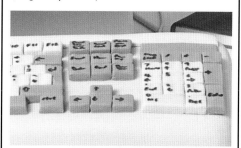

each key. Darken a small amount of modelling paste and make the darker keys, some of which you will have to cut with a knife as their sizes vary. Stick all the keys in position and, once they are secure, write on them using a black food pen.

Mouse

Take 60g (2oz) of grey modelling paste and, using Template 1 (see page 95), model into a rough mouse shape. Trim the paste to shape. Place the mouse on its side on Template 2 (see page 95), shape the top and cut the excess paste away from the base. To define the buttons, cut into the paste with a craft knife.

Mug

1. Roll the pale brown modelling paste into a 3.5cm (1³/₈") wide cylinder, then cut it to a length of 4.5cm (1³/₄"). Stand the cylinder on one of the cut ends and leave to dry. Cut a rectangle 11cm (4¼") long 5cm (2") wide) from white modelling paste and wrap it around the cylinder to make the outside edge of the mug. Neatly secure, then gently ease the top of the mug outwards to make the lip (see photograph).

2. Model a handle from white modelling paste using the template as a guide (see page 95) and leave to dry. Decorate the mug using flowerpaste, then attach the handle with sugar glue. Colour the run out icing so that it looks like tea or coffee, then pour it into the top of the mug and allow to dry.

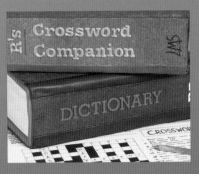

Materials

35.5cm x 30.5cm (14"x 12")
oblong cake drum
23cm x 28cm (9"x11") oblong
Madeira cake
Buttercream
2.24kg (5lb) sugarpaste
2 x 30.5cm x 25.5cm (12"x10")
hardboard cake boards or
pastillage (for making the
book covers)
1.236kg (2lb 12oz)
Mexican Modelling Paste (MMP),
coloured as follows:
168g (6oz) red (SK Poppy)
168g (6oz) dark green (SK
Holly/Ivy)
450g(1lb) blue (SK Wisteria)
450g(1lb) green (SK Mint)
Paste colours to colour the
above, plus:
Black
Yellow (SK Sunflower)
Green (SK Fern and Cactus)
Squires Kitchen Edible Lustre Dust:
Gold
Pastillage, small amount (for the
pencil)
Gildesol, Sugar glue

Equipment

Pair of smoothers
Plastic cutting strip (from a cling
film box or similar)
Straight edge, e.g. a ruler
Sugar shaper
Paintbrushes
Natural sponge
Ribbon
Letter cutters or piping tube
Food pens, including italics: black

TEMPLATE USED

Crosswords

The first crossword puzzle was published in a Sunday supplement of the New York World in December 1913. It became a regular feature and gradually other Sunday and later many daily newspapers worldwide began to publish crosswords. Definite rules both for construction and solutions developed, as did the number of forms a crossword might take. Crosswords are designed to entertain as well as to inform, which is probably why they appeal to so many newspaper and periodical readers. I have designed this cake for my father, who became hooked a number of years ago when The Daily Telegraph ran a series explaining how to solve its more challenging cryptic crosswords.

Covering the Board

1. Colour 1.12kg (2lb 8oz) sugarpaste a very pale warm grey, using a touch of black and yellow, and cover the board.

2. Trim the sides, then take the plastic cutting strip from a cling film box and press it into the paste 0.75cm (¼") from one of the shorter edges. Then place the strip a fraction nearer the outside and

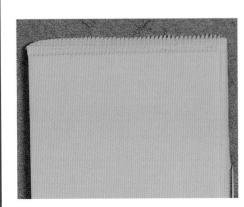

press again. Continue in this fashion until you reach the edge: it should now resemble the pages of a newspaper.

3. Take a straight edge and press it 0.5cm (³/₁₆") in from the long left-hand edge. Repeat a number of times until you reach the edge of the board. Leave to dry.

4. Draw the crossword design and newsprint onto the board with food pens, using an italic pen to draw the thin lines of the crossword grid (S.E.pp.79 & 95). There is a lot of scope here for personalising your cake.

The Books

1. Level the cake to a height of 5cm (2"), then cut out two 21cm x 26cm (8¼"x 10¼") oblongs and place each on waxed paper.

Roland's
Crossword
Companion
NEW EDITION
R's
Crossword
Companion
LMS
DICTIONARY
RB
CROSSWORD 1931

2. Spread a layer of buttercream over one of the oblong cakes then cover it with white sugarpaste. Use a pair of smoothers held at right angles to one another to make the edges of the book as sharp as possible: gently ease the paste up and across to the corners to eliminate the curved edges. Take a straight edge and press it repeatedly into the paste to mark the book's pages on the short and one of the longer sides. Repeat for the second book and allow to dry.

Book Covers

You can use either pastillage or hardboard cake boards to make these. Make or cut four 14.5cm x 22.5cm (5³/₄" x 8⁷/₈") rectangular book covers. Then cut four 2cm (3/4") wide strips from thinly rolled red modelling paste. Glue these over and along the shorter edges of two of the book covers as in Fig.1. In the same manner, make and glue green strips on to the other two book covers. Allow to dry.

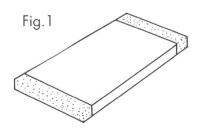

Fig.1

1. Lower Cover: Cut 2cm (³/₄") wide strips from thinly rolled blue modelling paste and place on top of the red (Fig.2), bringing the paste over the long edge. Turn the cover over and place on a smaller object, taking care not to flatten any of the soft paste. Next, completely cover the side that is uppermost with blue modelling paste and bring the paste over the long edge, trimming and blending

it with the paste below. Cut the sides fractionally in from the edges to reveal the red beneath. Repeat with green modelling paste for the other book. Leave to dry.

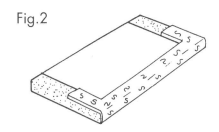

Fig.2

2. Spine: Once thoroughly dry, turn the blue book cover over onto a flat surface. Remove one of the cakes from its waxed paper and carefully place it onto the cover, ensuring that the back of the cake is in line with the uncovered edge of the cover. Place the top book cover in position on top of the cake, again ensuring that it is in line: check this with a smoother. Fill any gaps you may have with white sugarpaste trimmings so that you have a smooth foundation to your spine. Next, cut out a strip of red modelling paste, approximately 6cm x 22.5cm (2³/₈" x 8⁷/₈"), and attach it in position, smoothing the edges where they join the book covers. Repeat for the green book.

3. Upper cover: Cut 2cm (³/₄") wide strips from thinly rolled blue modelling paste, carefully lift the book cover and stick these strips in the same position as the lower ones, smoothing all joins. Then completely cover the upper cover, bringing the paste over the long edge and trimming and blending it with paste below. As before, cut the sides fractionally shorter than the red paste beneath. Trim the paste that meets the binding

neatly, then smooth to eliminate the cut edge.

4. Cut a strip of blue modelling paste to cover the spine. Blend in the top edge with the paste of the cover.

5. Cut strips of thin paste to go over the corners of the spine and glue in place to give the book a neat appearance.

6. Repeat steps 3, 4 and 5 for the green book.

7. Painting: Dilute some blue paste colour in clear spirit and sponge paint the cover of the blue book. Touch up the tricky areas with a stiff-bristled brush. Repeat for the green book and allow to dry. With some extremely dilute brown/black, paint over the pages of the books, bringing the pages to life.

8. Lettering (S.E.p.79): Make letters for the book titles, another opportunity to personalise the cake. Gild the letters, if desired, using Gildesol and edible lustre dust. Then carefully glue in position, adding detail with a food pen.

Assembling the Cake

Make a pencil, then place all in position on the board. The top book, because of the rigidity of its cover, can be placed at any angle, so experiment. Once you are happy, secure all the pieces in position. Finally, attach a ribbon around the board. Remember to tell the crossword puzzler to lift the covers of the books before trying to cut the cakes!

SPECIAL *Effects* & *Accessories*

Lettering

There are numerous ways of applying lettering to cakes: which you chose depends very much on the result you require.

Letter Cutters:

A quick method as there are a number of letter cutters available on the market. To use letter cutters, press them into thinly rolled out flowerpaste or modelling paste. Once firm, the letters can be transferred to the cake.

Embossing:

Again a quick method with various embossers available. Take the embossers and carefully press them into soft sugarpaste. With some sets you have to emboss the letters individually (so take care to keep the letters straight), whilst with others the letters can be placed together before embossing. When dry, the embossed letters can be left as they are, painted or piped over.

Runouts:

A very versatile method as you can make any style and size of letter you wish. Choose a style of lettering and make a template. A computer is an excellent source of fonts and you have the added bonus of being able to make the letters any size you wish, but there are also many books on lettering. Place a piece of waxed paper over the template and outline each letter with royal icing using a No. 1 tube. Next, flood in the letters with softened royal icing. Allow the letters to dry thoroughly, then remove from the waxed paper and attach to the cake.

Pressure Piping:

Often used for more delicate lettering. Make a template as for the runout letters. Using a No. 1 tube and royal icing, pipe over the outline of the letters, but this time apply pressure in the thicker parts of the letters as you work. Allow to dry thoroughly before transferring to the cake.

Food Pens:

These are now available in the complete spectrum of colours and in both plain and italic nibs. They are excellent for freehand writing and very quick and easy to use. Make sure the sugar surface is dry, then use the pens as you would a felt tip.

Newsprint

The easiest way to make newspaper print is to copy the real thing! Start by selecting a suitable section from a newspaper and cutting it to the required size. If you wish to be accurate, trace the page onto dry sugarpaste as shown, then add the newsprint with a black food pen. You may find, however, that using the page just as a reference is all you need, but do try to keep your lines of print straight: a set square is very useful for this. Adding your own headlines can add an extra twist to the cake. Pictures are best painted with black paste colour diluted in clear spirit.

Pencil

Place some pastillage in a sugar shaper fitted with a hexagon disc. Push through about 1cm (3/8"), take hold off this and pull gently so that the pastillage elongates and breaks in two, leaving a pointed shape protruding from the shaper: the tip of the pencil. Extrude a pencil length of pastillage, place on foam, straighten and leave to dry. Dilute some green and brown paste colours in clear spirit and paint the pencil.

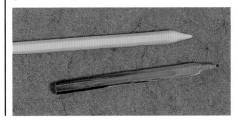

Materials

20cm (8") square Madeira cake
25cm (10") square cake drum
Buttercream
Sugarpaste:
672g (1½lb) pale terracotta
672g (1½lb) pale brown
Mexican Modelling Paste (MMP):
112g (4oz) white
56g (2oz) green
112g (4oz) terracotta
140g (5oz) flesh
Flowerpaste:
15g (½oz) black
28g (1oz) pale brown
28g (1oz) dark blue (SK Bluebell),
15g (½oz) cream
28g (1 oz) white
Paste colours:
browns (e.g. SK Terracotta and
Chestnut), black, white
Colours of your choice to paint the face
Colours of your choice to paint the
magazines
Dust colours: pale peach
Squires Kitchen Edible Lustre Dusts:
Silver and Gold
Clear spirit, e.g. vodka or gin
Gildesol, Sugar glue, Spaghetti/sugar
sticks

Equipment

Waxed paper, Smoothers, Spacers
Straight edge, e.g. ruler
Dresden tool, Ball tool
Paintbrushes
Sponge (for painting the worktop)
Circle cutters:
4.5cm (1¾")
3.5cm (1 3/8"), 2.5cm (1")
2cm (¾")
Polystyrene block
Medium-sized female template (see
page 97), Holly Products Adult Head
Mould, Barbecue skewers (to help
support the figure on the polystyrene)
Foam (to support the figure)
Strip cutters, including narrow and
decorative (for decorating the cake)
Food pens:
red (SK Poinsettia)
dark blue (SK Bluebell)
black (SK Blackberry)
dark red (SK Cyclamen)

Sugarcraft

Originally, the only source of sweetening available to man was honey. Nevertheless, the history of sugarcraft can be traced back at least 3000 years to Egyptian hieroglyphics, which indicate that the art of sugar confectionery was then well established. By the fourteenth century, moulded sugar was being used for display purposes. In the sixteenth century, sugar became available in increasing quantities from the West Indies and, from the 1540s, due to the refinement of sugar in London, a range of sweet products became available. Sugar moulding became popular, with animals and fruit being cast in sugar or moulded from marzipan. Wine glasses were also made from sugarplate, a crisp, modelled sugar. In the eighteenth and nineteenth centuries, European confectioners made sugar flowers from gum paste very much in the way they are made now. Today, sugar is available to all and sugarcraft has become an absorbing and satisfying hobby for many of us.

The Figure

NOTE: It is particularly important with this figure that you allow sufficient time for the modelling paste to dry thoroughly: a week in a warm, dry place such as an airing cupboard would be ideal.

For detailed instructions on how to make the body parts, please refer to the Figure Modelling section on pages 92-93.

1. Legs: To make the legs, use the medium-sized female template (see page 94) and refer to the instructions on page 93. This time, however, once you have made the tapered sausage and before shaping the ankle and knee, shape the foot and insert a length of spaghetti or a sugar stick down through the length of the leg to protrude from the heel. Once both legs are shaped, insert the spaghetti/sugar sticks protruding from the heels into the polystyrene block so that the legs are standing on the block hip-width apart. Position the legs so that they look natural and the feet are flat. Allow to dry thoroughly.

2. Torso: Model the torso and carefully attach it to the legs with sugar glue. Insert barbecue skewers into the polystyrene at the back and front of the figure in order to help support the torso in position on top of the legs whilst it dries.

3. Head: Model the head using the medium-sized head mould and manipulate it to create a suitable expression (see page 92). Once

80

81

the head has dried, add the ears, then paint and dust the facial detail. Place to one side.

4. Shoes: Thinly roll out some dark brown flowerpaste (SK Bulrush) and cover the front of each foot, trimming the paste to shape with small scissors. Next, cut two small strips and wrap one around the heel of each shoe.

5. Trousers: Paint sugar glue along one inside leg and around half of the waist. Roll out a rectangle of light brown paste approximately 8cm x 12cm ($3^1/_4$"x $4^3/_4$"). Exact measurements are not necessary as the paste is cut to shape on the figure. Place one of the long edges on the inside leg and shape the paste around the leg, allowing it some fullness. Trim the excess

paste on the inside leg seam with scissors and the waist and front and back seams with a cutting wheel. Repeat for the other leg and allow to dry.

TIP: Now is probably the best time to cover the cake as the figure should be reasonably solid and because doing so will enable you to position the figures arms accurately.

6. Remove the figure from the polystyrene and cut the spaghetti/sugar stick flush with the soles of the feet. Place the figure in position on the cake, but do not stick in place: it is probably a good idea to support her with foam to prevent any mishaps. Model both arms and attach them to the body, positioning them on the work surface as desired. Once

the paste holds its shape, remove the figure from the cake and place it in a warm, dry environment to dry thoroughly. This will prevent the arms from falling off when

7. Shirt Sleeves: Thinly roll out a rectangle of dark blue flowerpaste (SK Bluebell). Roughly pleat the paste as shown, then cut into two smaller rectangles and wrap one around each arm from the elbow upwards. Trim the under arm seam with scissors and around the shoulders with a cutting wheel.

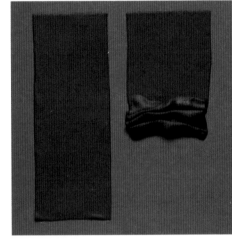

8. Shirt: Cut two 9cm x 6cm ($3^1/_2$"x $2^1/_4$") rectangles from the blue flowerpaste. Paint glue around the top of each arm and down the underarm seam. With the 2cm ($3/_4$") circle cutter, remove a half circle of paste to make the neck on one of the 6cm ($2^1/_4$") edges of each rectangle. Place the front of the shirt in position, trimming it to shape at the shoulders and sides with a cutting wheel. Make the back in the same manner, ensuring that the length of the hem is the same as at the front. Press the paste into her waist to form folds and give a close fit.

9. Apron: Cut strips from white flowerpaste using a narrow strip cutter. Place one around her waist, then make a bow and tails and stick onto the back of the waist. Next, loop a short strip around her neck. Cut the apron front from white flowerpaste, taking the dimensions from the figure, and secure in position. Once dry, decorate the apron using food pens (a chance to personalise the cake).

10. Secure the figure in position on the cake using thick sugar glue. Then stick the head in position, adjusting the cut of the neck with a craft knife if necessary. Make the hair by placing some softened brown modelling paste and mesh disc in a sugar shaper and extruding lengths of paste. Attach these to the head with sugar glue in your chosen style.

Covering the Board

Cover the board with the pale terracotta sugarpaste and indent the lines for the floor tiles with the straight edge. Allow to dry. Dilute some brown and cream paste colours with clear spirit and dab randomly over the tiles (see below). Mix up some light grey colour and paint the lines between the tiles.

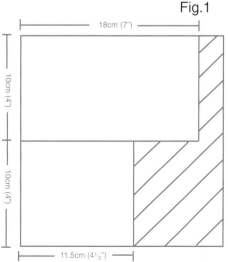

Fig.1

18cm (7")

10cm (4")

10cm (4")

11.5cm (4½")

Carving and Covering the Cake

1. Level the cake to a height of 6.3cm (2½"), then cut as shown in Fig.1. Place the two required sections of cake on their sides on waxed paper to form kitchen units with a height of 10cm (4").

2. Roll out the pale brown sugarpaste between spacers and cut rectangles to fit the two inner sides of the cake, the sides where the figure stands. Stick these in position with buttercream and use a smoother to ensure that they are flush both with the sides and with the top of the cake. Next, cut a rectangle to fit the front of the cake (the side with the stack of drawers) and secure in position. Then cut and secure rectangles to fit the remaining long side, followed by the two end sections.

3. Roll out the remaining pale brown sugarpaste and cut a rectangle fractionally larger than the length and width of the front work surface. Gently round all the cut edges, except for where the second work surface abuts, and secure in place with buttercream. Cut a second rectangle for the remaining worktop area and secure in position. Allow to dry.

4. Dilute some brown paste colour (SK Chestnut) in clear spirit and apply a vertically streaked colour wash to the sides of all the units. Colour the work surface by sponge painting with a variety of diluted colours (I used the same colours as for the floor). Have a go and experiment: if you are not happy, wipe it off and start again. Do not worry about the surface of the paste as work surfaces are frequently textured.

5. Roll out the terracotta modelling paste and cut out the drawers, six measuring 6cm x 1.7cm (2 $^3/_8$" x $^5/_8$") and one measuring 4cm x 1.7cm (11/2" x 5/8"). Then cut out the doors, six measuring 6cm x 7cm (2 $^3/_8$" x 2 $^3/_4$") and one measuring 4cm x 7cm(1 $^1/_2$"x 2 $^3/_4$"). Stick these in position as shown. The 4cm (1 $^1/_2$") wide door and drawer are placed on the inner rear side.

6. Dilute some terracotta paste colour in clear spirit and apply a vertically streaked colour wash to all the doors and drawers. Allow to dry.

7. To make the handles, roll out some white modelling paste and cut into 2cm ($^3/_4$") wide rectangles. Shape these with a 3.5cm (1 $^3/_8$") circle cutter as

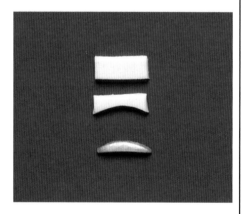

shown and secure in position with sugar glue. Once dry, paint all the handles with silver lustre dust mixed with clear spirit.

Assembling the Cake
Make your chosen accessories (S.E.pp.84-85). Place on the cake. Once you are happy with their positions, secure with sugar glue.

SPECIAL *Effects* *& Accessories*

All the accessories are ones I use when cake decorating. They have been made to $^1/_8$th scale, so if you have other items you would like to include, remember to scale the dimensions down accordingly.

Cake Tin
Thinly roll out some white flowerpaste and cut out a 3.5cm (1 $^3/_8$") circle and a 11cm x 1.25cm (4 $^1/_4$" x $^1/_2$") strip. Leave the strip on the board to harden slightly, then wrap it around the circle as shown. Once dry, apply a layer of Gildesol, then dust with silver lustre dust.

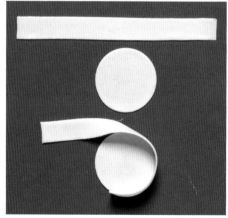

Cake
Thinly roll out some white modelling paste for the cake drum and cut a 4.5cm (1$^3/_4$") circle. Next, thickly roll out some more

modelling paste and cut out the cake with a 3.5cm (1$^3/_8$") cutter. I have made my cake the equivalent of two cakes stacked on top of one another for impact. Place the cake centrally on the board and allow to dry. To decorate the cake, use dark blue flowerpaste (SK Bluebell) and a decorative strip cutter (see below). Pipe small beads of let-down white sugarpaste and, once dry, gild with gold lustre dust mixed with clear spirit. Finish the cake by adding an inscription with a food pen.

Paint Palette
Cut a 2.5cm (1") circle from modelling paste and indent the holes with a ball tool.

Mixer & Mixing Bowl

Cut a shape 5cm (2") long, 2cm (3/4") wide and 2cm (3/4") high from white modelling paste. Cut away the area where the bowl will sit (see photograph). Place a square of grey modelling paste on top of the white as illustrated. Cut

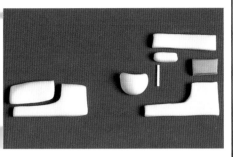

an oblong 1cm (3/8") deep x 4cm (1 1/2") long x 1.75cm (5/8") wide from white modelling paste. Allow to dry before placing in position on top of the mixer. Make a mixing bowl from a small ball of paste, using a ball tool to create the centre. Model the trimmings as shown and assemble the mixer.

Towels

Roll out some flowerpaste very thinly and cut out rectangles. For the white towel, cut narrow strips of thinly rolled dark blue

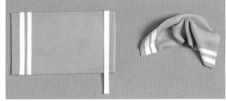

flowerpaste and place around the edges of the towel. Trim the strips to size and texture with a piece of foam. Carefully pick up each towel by the centre of one of the longer sides and position on the cake: if the paste is thin enough, it should easily hang in folds. Adjust as necessary.

Additional Accessories

Make the green work board, dust pots, rolling pin, spacers and sugar shaker from appropriately coloured modelling paste, dividing all dimensions by eight.
Model the smoothers, modelling tools, cutters, magazines and flowerpaste packet from suitably coloured flowerpaste. Once dry, decorate them with food pens and diluted paste and dust colours.

Materials

41cm (16") oval cake drum
A 7 egg Madeira cake split and
cooked between a 30cm x 20cm
(12"x 8") oblong tin and a 8cm
(3¼") round tin
Buttercream
Paste colours: black, yellow, red,
blue and brown
2.6kg (5lb 8oz) sugarpaste,
coloured as follows:
960g (2lb) dark grey
480g (1lb) black
480g (1lb) yellow (SK Sunflower,
plus a little Marigold)
120g (4oz) red
240g (8oz) blue (SK Hydrangea,
with a touch of Wisteria)
240g (8oz) white 60g (2oz) light
brown (SK Teddy Bear Brown)
60g (2oz) dark brown (SK Bulrush)
Dust colour: black/
(SK Smokey Haze)
Squires Kitchen Edible Lustre Dust:
Silver
Royal icing
240g (8oz) pastillage
15g (½oz) caster sugar, Gildesol
Sugar sticks: 14cm (5½"), 10cm
(4") and 2 x 4cm (1½")

Equipment

Knife (for carving the cake)
Small plastic bag (for colouring the
caster sugar)
Rolling pin, Smoother
Circle cutters: 6cm (2⅜"), 4.5cm
(1¾"), 3.5cm (1⅜"), 2.5cm (1")
and 2cm (¾")
Waxed paper
Ball tool, Dresden tool
Sugar shaper, Wooden dowel
Number and letter cutters
Ribbon (to go around the board)

TEMPLATES USED

Karting

Karting is a very exciting and relatively inexpensive form of motor sport, popular ever since the American Art Ingels first invented the karts in 1957. They are the first cars most people learn to race and many famous Rally and F1 drivers have learnt their skill in these vehicles.

Covering the Board

Cover the board with dark grey sugarpaste and texture with coloured caster sugar to give the effect of a track (S.E.p.89).

Carving the Cake

You will probably find it best to freeze the cake first and carve while frozen.

1. Level the oblong cake, place Template No.1 (see page 96) on top and cut around the kart.

2. Cut out the cubes of cake that make the wheels, turn these on their sides and shape using a 4.5cm (1¾") circle cutter for the rear wheels and a 3.5cm (1⅜")

circle cutter for the front wheels. Take sections from the middle of each wheel using 2.5cm (1") and 2cm (¾") circle cutters respectively. Cover and place to one side.

86

3. Cut the side kart sections away from the main body of the kart and level to a height of 4cm (1½"). Likewise, cut away the front of the kart, shaping it from a height of 4cm (1½") at its sides to 3cm (1¼") at its front. Curve each front edge and place the carved pieces to one side.

4. Cut the base of the kart to a height of 2cm (¾"), level the engine and shape the tank between the driver's legs.

5. Using the templates (see page 96) and photographs as a guide, start carving the figure from his feet upwards. Once you get to his middle, insert the 14cm (5½") sugar stick into the base cake and place the round cake on top: this will give your figure more support. Continue to carve the body, finishing with his helmet.

6. Position the main body of the kart on the board.

7. Make the following pastillage pieces: Bumper and Pedals, Steering Wheel, Front Number panel (S.E.p.89) and the Driver's Arms as follows.

Driver's Arms
Using Template No.2 (see page 96) and the carved cake as a guide, model arms from 3cm (1¼") balls of white pastillage. Once you are happy with their shape, make a hole in the shoulder joint with the blunt end of a wooden dowel, then leave overnight to dry. Place sugar sticks into these holes, securing them with royal icing as illustrated.

Covering the Cake
NOTE: Use buttercream to stick the sugarpaste to the cake, spreading it thinly over the part you are about to cover.

Cover the base of the kart with black sugarpaste. It is easiest to do this in sections, blending joins in the paste together when all sections are in place. Cover the tank between the driver's legs with white sugarpaste, then insert a 10cm (4") sugar stick at an 50 degree angle to act as the steering column. Secure with royal icing.

The Racing Driver
1. Legs: If necessary, add small amounts of sugarpaste to build up and give more definition to the legs. Cover one leg at a time with blue sugarpaste. Trim the paste to fit first the inner leg and then the outer. Take a ball tool and push it into and along the paste to give movement to the fabric. Soften some white sugarpaste and place it with the smallest ribbon disc in a sugar shaper. Extrude a length and attach this down the sides of each trouser leg, remembering to work the strip into the creases of the fabric with a ball tool.

2. Lower Body: The body is covered in two halves, front and back, thereby creating shoulder and side seams. Cover the entire front and half of the back with blue sugarpaste, trim and neaten the seams. Smooth the upper cut edge of the paste on the back.

3. Arms: Cover the pastillage arms with blue sugarpaste then, as for the trousers, give the paste some movement with a ball tool and add white stripes. Use a wooden dowel to make holes in the body where the arms are to be attached, fill these with royal icing, then push the arms into position. If necessary, support on pieces of foam until the royal icing is dry.

4. Upper Body: Attach a band of white sugarpaste followed by a red one to the upper body and shoulders, attaching the front and back sections separately as before. Give movement to the fabric with a ball tool. Then, if desired, trim the driver's top with paste extruded from a sugar shaper.

5. Head: Make a sausage of yellow sugarpaste and fit it around the driver's neck. Roll out some yellow sugarpaste and use it to cover the helmet. Smooth around the base of the helmet and pull up a pleat at the front. Cut away the pleat and rub the join closed, trim around the base. Cut a visor from grey sugarpaste (Template 7, page 96) and secure in position. Paint the visor with diluted black paste. Lastly, add designs of your choice to the helmet.

6. Feet: Take two 1cm (³/₈") balls of light brown sugarpaste and shape into boots. Thinly roll some dark brown sugarpaste, cut soles and laces for the boots and attach with sugar glue. Position on the kart. Take two 1cm (³/₈") balls of red sugarpaste, roll into small fat sausages and place between the end of the trousers and the boots. Texture by making small cuts in different directions with the sharper end of a Dresden tool. Insert the brake and accelerator pedals into the cake at the ends of the feet.

7. Hands: Secure the steering wheel in position with a small amount of royal icing. Next, model gloves from light brown sugarpaste by the method used for making hands (see Figure Modelling on pages 92-93). Fix onto the ends of the pastillage arms, adjusting the fingers so that they rest in a comfortable driving position on the steering wheel. Roll out some red sugarpaste and cut strips to go around each arm. Glue into position and texture with a Dresden tool.

The Kart
1. Seat: Cover the seat with white sugarpaste. Trim the edges with black sugarpaste extruded from a sugar shaper fitted with a large round disc.

2. Engine: Add some white sugarpaste to the grey sugarpaste trimmings to make a light grey paste. Roll this out and cover the top of the engine, then cut and place a strip around the sides. To disguise the join between the two, make and glue in position black strips made with a sugar shaper fitted with the smallest round disc. Next, model a 4.5cm (1 3/4") ball of grey paste, elongate it slightly and cut it in half so that it fits neatly on top of engine box. Then use a knife to mark a radial pattern and glue in position. Model other engine parts, pipes and hoses from grey sugarpaste and secure in place with sugar glue. (Unless you are making this cake for a real enthusiast, the engine details need not be technically correct: the idea is to give the impression of an engine.)

3. Wheels: Cover the four wheels (S.E.p.91). Place the wheels in position, together with axles modelled from grey paste.

4. Kart Body: Place the carved front of the kart in position and cover with buttercream. Roll out some yellow sugarpaste, cutting a straight line across the top of the paste. Pick up the paste and place this straight edge where the uncovered cake meets the covered black base. Gently ease the paste over the cake and cut off the excess. Spread the sides of the kart with buttercream, then completely cover them with yellow sugarpaste. Carefully lift and place in position. Add designs of your choice to the kart.

Assembling the Cake

1. Edge the entire cake with a thin strip of black sugarpaste to neaten the join between the board and cake. Fix the bumper in position with royal icing. Insert the front number panel into the cake in front of the steering column at an angle of 45 degrees and secure with royal icing.

2. Finally, attach a length of ribbon around the board.

Road

Colour some sugarpaste dark grey. Place some caster sugar and black dust colour (SK Smokey Haze) in a small plastic bag and shake so that the dust colours the sugar. Make the road with dark grey sugarpaste, then sprinkle the coloured sugar over the surface. Using a smoother, gently press the sugar into the paste, adding more sugar if necessary to give the road depth and texture.

Bumper & Pedals

Place some softened white pastillage and the medium-sized round disc in a sugar shaper. Lay the bumper template (No.6, page 96) under some waxed paper and extrude pastillage over the lines of the template. Leave overnight to dry. Work some Gildesol over the surface of the bumper, then apply silver lustre dust. Make the brake and accelerator pedals in exactly the same way.

Steering Wheel

Roll out some white pastillage and cut out the central section of the steering wheel (Template No.4, page 96). Colour a small amount of pastillage black and place it in a sugar shaper together with the largest round disc. Extrude enough to go around the edge of the steering wheel, then place a 6cm (2³/₈") circle cutter over the central section and use it to guide the black paste into a circle. Leave to dry overnight. Attach small balls of black paste as illustrated, topping the central one with a yellow ball. Work some Gildesol over the surface of the white pastillage, then apply silver lustre dust.

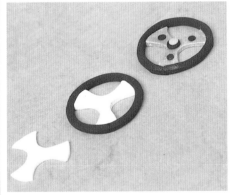

Front Number Panel

Colour some pastillage yellow then, using Template No.5 (see page 96), cut out the required shape. Leave to dry overnight. As coloured pastillage will dry lighter than sugarpaste of the same colour, cover the front of this piece with yellow sugarpaste leaving

2cm (3/4") of the lower edge uncovered. Add your choice of numbers, securing them in place with a little sugar glue.

Wheels

Roll out a piece of black sugarpaste large enough to cover one of the wheels completely. Place the front of the wheel into the middle of the paste, bring the

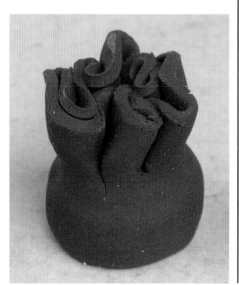

paste up around the side and squeeze it together at the top. Cut off the excess paste and smooth the rear side of the wheel. Turn the wheel over and, using a ball tool,

gently ease the paste into the recessed centre.

Smooth the front of the wheel and then its edges by rolling it along the work surface. Using a small

circle cutter, cut out a yellow centre for the wheel, glue in position and smooth to shape with a ball tool.

Glue a small black ball to the centre of the wheel and attach a length of grey sugarpaste for the wheel trim (silver lustre dust can be applied).

MORE SPECIAL Effects

Chequered Flag

Cut a flag from thinly rolled white flowerpaste. Cut small squares from black flowerpaste and glue to the flag in a chequered pattern. Leave to dry over an uneven surface to give movement.

Figure Modelling

This is not as daunting as it may first appear. Using a mould to construct the basic face shape you can, with a little practice, achieve some very realistic results - you will even find that people recognise themselves!
Although the figures in this book all use body templates and Holly Products Adult Head Moulds, it helps to be aware of some basics when modelling.

1. Generally, an adult's height is equivalent to seven adult heads, although this can vary from five to eight heads.

2. A shoulder width is twice the length of the head.

3. Elbows are at waist height.

4. The length of the foot is equal to the length of head.

5. The measurement from knee to ankle bone is equal to that from elbow to knuckle.

6. The length of a hand should equal the length from the chin to the middle of the forehead. The length of a hand should be twice its width.

When modelling someone's likeness, I like, ideally, to have a good full length photo so that I can measure their proportions and a good close up of their face to enable me to achieve a reasonable likeness of their face shape and features.

Head

1. Knead some flesh-coloured modelling paste, adding a trace of white fat. Make a ball of a suitable size and press it firmly into the chosen head mould (i.e. small, medium or large). Shape the back of the head: do not worry about any marks in the paste as these will be covered later by the hair. Remove the head from the mould.

2. Working by hand and with a Dresden tool, start manipulating the face into the shape required. I usually begin by extending the chin, stroking the paste from under the chin forwards and pinching it into

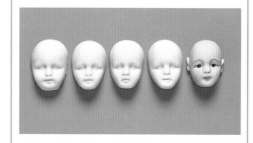

shape. Bear in mind that male chins are more pronounced than female ones.

3. Define the cheeks by pressing a Dresden tool in a diagonal from the nostril to the side of the mouth. Gently smooth the paste of the cheeks into the correct position for the chosen expression. I often find it helps to have a willing volunteer at this stage!

4. Open and extend the mouth with a knife, 'U' or Dresden tool, depending on the shape required. Insert a fine point into a nostril and gently circle to enlarge; repeat on the other side.

5. Adjust the eyes as necessary using a Dresden tool: I often push the lids of the lower eye up slightly and define the eye brows. Note that male eyebrows are more prominent than female ones.

6. Once you are happy with the shape of the head, cut off the neck, insert a piece of uncooked spaghetti or a sugar stick and leave to dry.

7. Add a very thin strip of white paste for the teeth and thin flesh-coloured strips for the upper eyelids.

Face

To paint the face, dilute suitable paste colours in clear spirit and use a fine paintbrush (e.g. No. 00) to paint the detail. It helps to have a clear photograph or a large picture of a face from a magazine at hand for reference: this way, the fine details of the mouth and eyes can be seen more clearly.

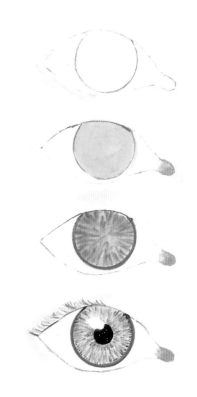

Eyes

Start by painting the whites of the eyes (the mould indicates where these should be), then paint the background colour of the iris (e.g. a pale brown or blue). Next, add details to the iris, such as a dark rim around the outside and radial flecks of different colours. Paint the pupil in the centre of the eye and, once dry, paint white light spots, ensuring that they are the same on each eye. Add a small dot of pink to the inner corner of each eye to mark the tear ducts. Paint the eyelashes, eyebrows, lips and, finally, brush the cheeks with skin tone/pink dust colours.

Ears

Take two small balls of paste and stick one on each side of the head. The tops of the ears should be in line with the eyebrows and the earlobes in line with the tip of the nose. To shape the ear, press the broader end of a Dresden tool onto the central portion of the ball and drag it carefully downwards, then sideways so that the central edge of the ball is blended into the face and the remaining paste forms a 'C' shape. Press the sharper end of a Dresden tool into the ear to form the ear canal.

Hair

There are a number of ways of creating hair:

1. *Pipe with a large plain tube (e.g. No. 4) and royal icing or let-down sugarpaste.*

2. *Push softened sugarpaste through a sugar shaper fitted with a mesh disc. This method is particularly useful for girls with long hair.*

3. *Texture modelling paste. To do this, cut out a fairly thick circle of*

hair-coloured modelling paste, remove 1/4 and stick the remaining paste to the head. Then texture the hair with a circle cutter and make a fringe, if required, from small pieces of textured paste. Alternatively, use a circle cutter to texture small amounts of rolled out paste and stick these to the head in overlapping layers. This is more time consuming, but makes styling the hair easier.

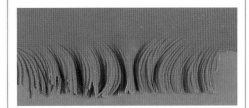

Torso

Use the appropriate template and model some flesh-coloured modelling paste to the correct shape. If you are making a female figure, you will find it much easier to add her breasts separately. Insert pieces of uncooked spaghetti or sugar sticks into the arm sockets and through the body: these will help to support the arms and head. Dry in an upright position.

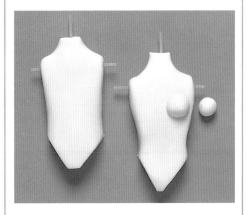

Legs

Make a tapered sausage that roughly fits the template. Shape the ankle by rolling and thinning the paste. Form the foot by squeezing the paste and modelling it to shape. For the knee, gently roll the sausage diagonally above and below the

joint, then bend to the required position. Define leg muscles as necessary with a Dresden tool and cut the top of the leg so that it fits snugly into the torso. Allow to dry, preferably in position on the cake and, if necessary, supported by pieces of foam. Repeat for the second leg.

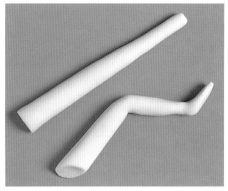

Arms

Make a tapered sausage of flesh-coloured modelling paste, then roll and thin the paste to shape the wrist and elbow using the template (see page 94) as a guide. Flatten the hand and, with a small pair of scissors, cut out a small triangle to form the thumb. Cut the fingers and gently roll to shape. Mark the fingernails with the tip of a Dresden tool and the knuckles with a knife. Cup the hand slightly with a ball tool. Repeat for the other arm. Cut the arms to fit onto the shoulder, glue in place, position and leave to dry.

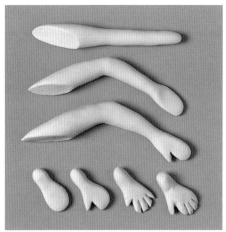

Figure Dressing

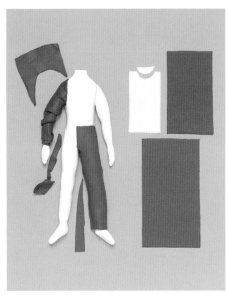

Dressing the Figures

The basic principles, shown here, of dressing the figures in this book are straight forward. The figures are all dressed using simple rectangle shapes: no detailed dress patterns are needed. The rectangles are simply placed in position and cut to shape using either a small pair of scissors (where the clothing joins to itself, e.g. the underarm seam) or a cutting wheel (where the clothing seams are on the body, e.g. the shoulder seam).

More detailed instructions can be found as follows: boots (Walking, pages 16-19), trousers (Sugarcraft, pages 80-85, or Gardening, pages 56-61) and shirts and jacket (Birdwatching 66-71).

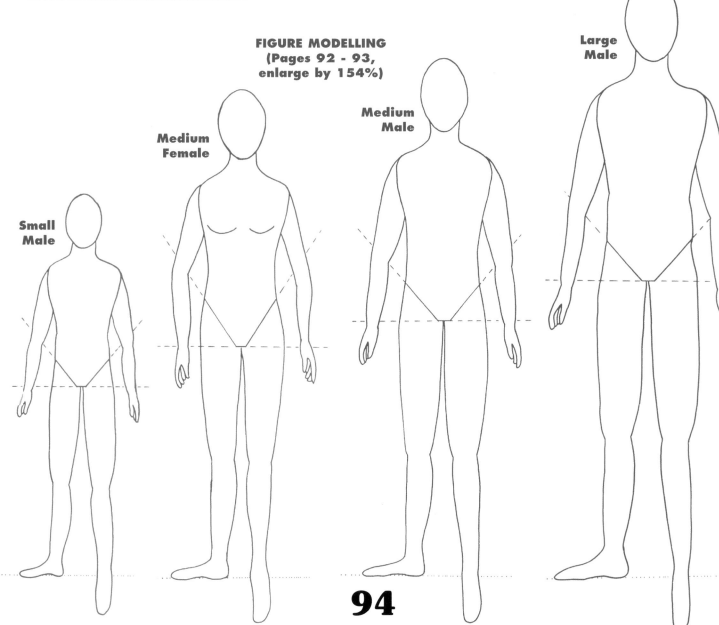

FIGURE MODELLING
(Pages 92 - 93,
enlarge by 154%)

Large Male

Medium Male

Medium Female

Small Male

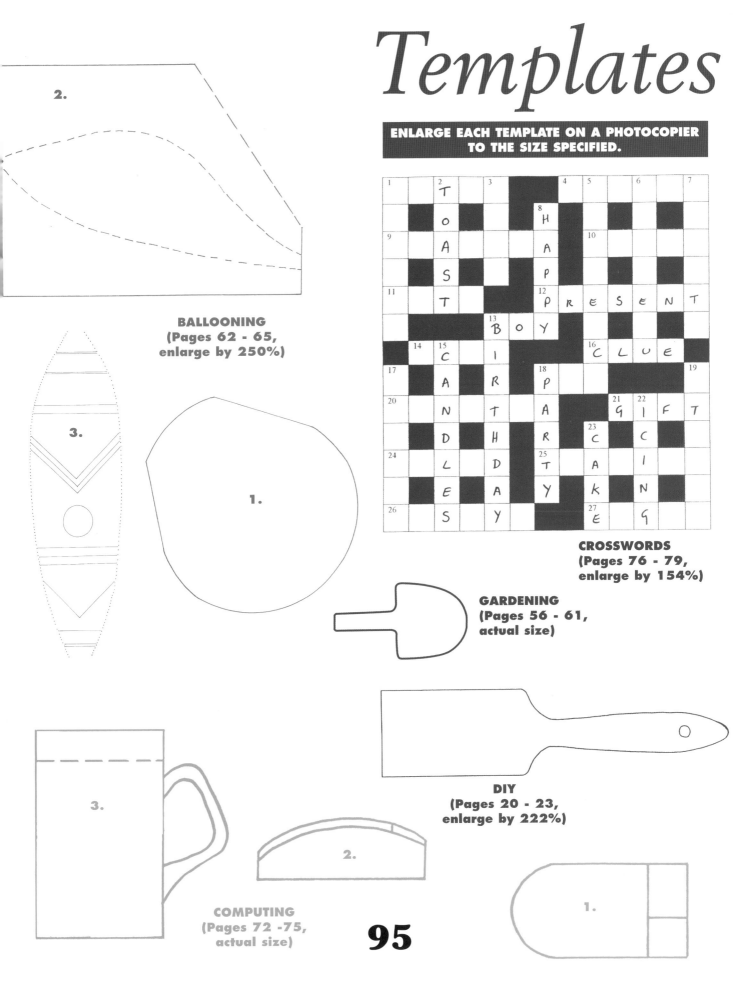

Templates

ENLARGE EACH TEMPLATE ON A PHOTOCOPIER TO THE SIZE SPECIFIED.

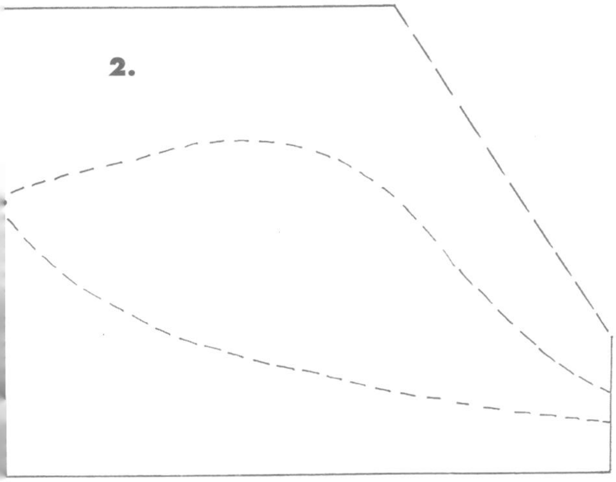

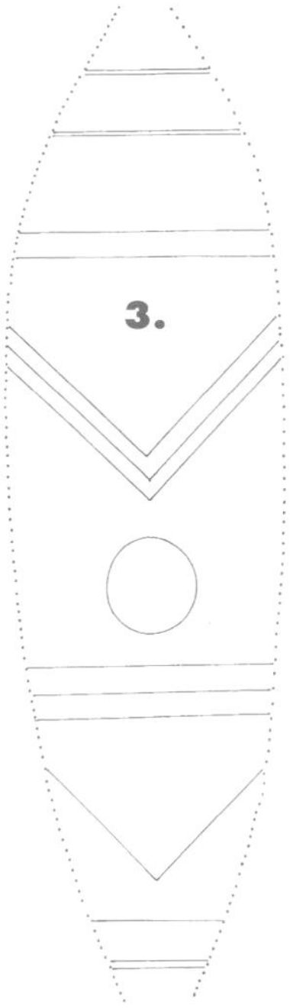

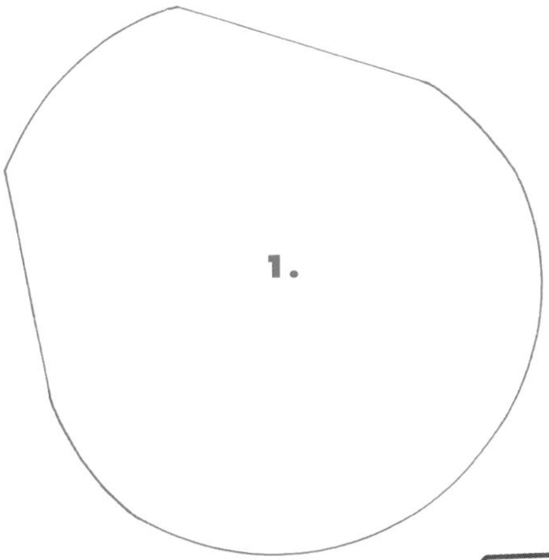

BALLOONING
(Pages 62 - 65, enlarge by 250%)

CROSSWORDS
(Pages 76 - 79, enlarge by 154%)

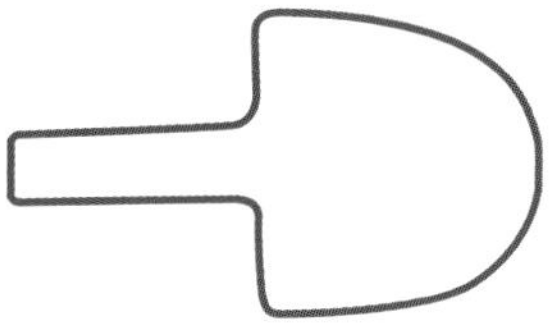

GARDENING
(Pages 56 - 61, actual size)

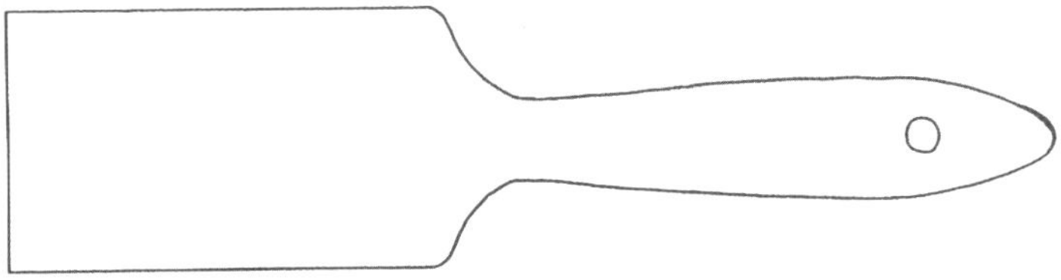

DIY
(Pages 20 - 23, enlarge by 222%)

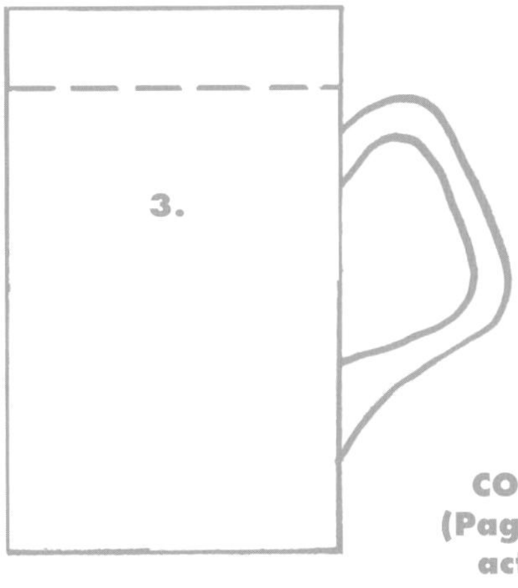

COMPUTING
(Pages 72 -75, actual size)

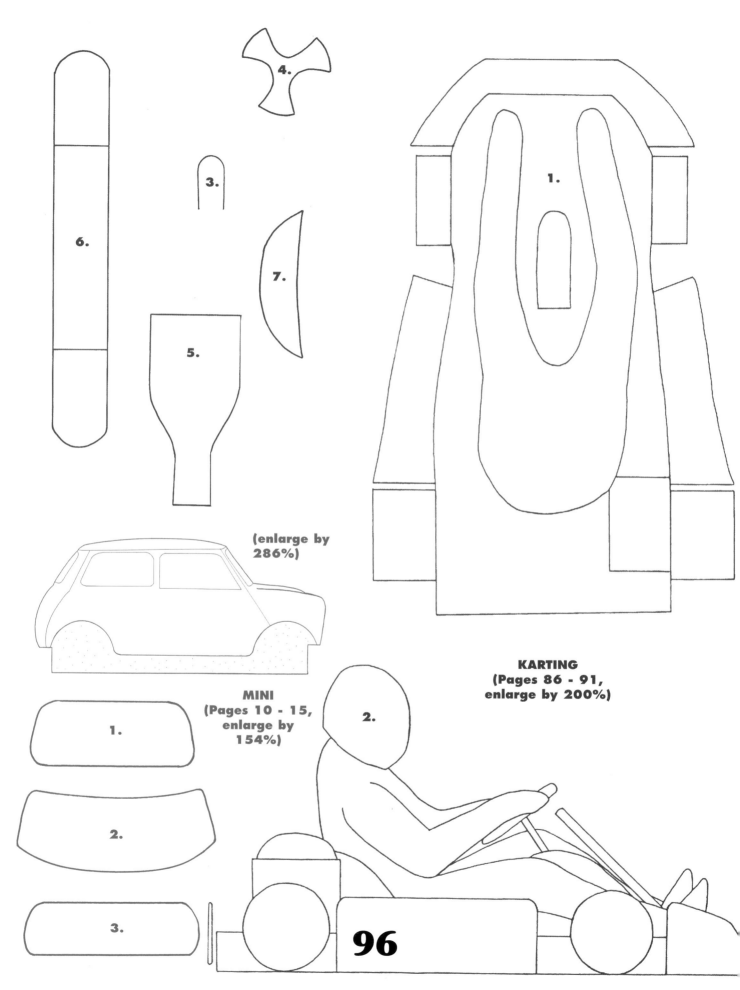

4.

3.

6.

7.

5.

1.

(enlarge by 286%)

KARTING
(Pages 86 - 91,
enlarge by 200%)

MINI
(Pages 10 - 15,
enlarge by
154%)

1.

2.

2.

3.

96

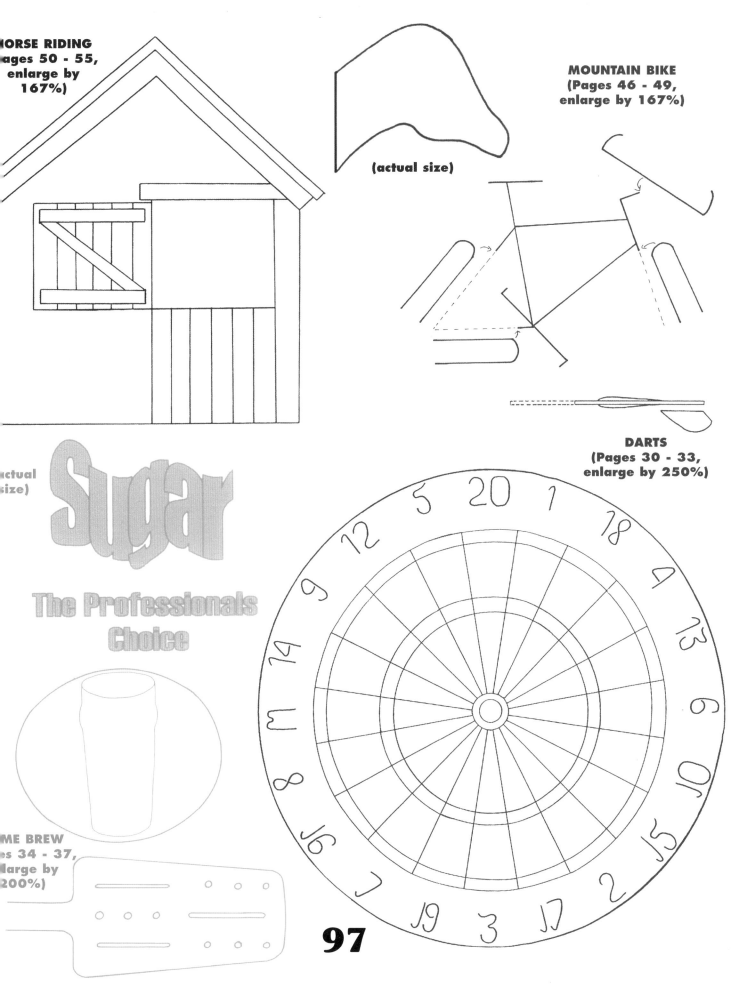

HORSE RIDING
(Pages 50 - 55,
enlarge by
167%)

MOUNTAIN BIKE
(Pages 46 - 49,
enlarge by 167%)

(actual size)

DARTS
(Pages 30 - 33,
enlarge by 250%)

(actual
size)

Sugar

The Professionals
Choice

HOME BREW
(Pages 34 - 37,
enlarge by
200%)

97

Index

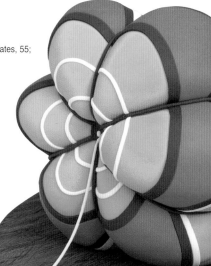

Notes

Notes